PIRATE

Manual

LOADS FOR YOUNG PIRATES TO MAKE AND DO

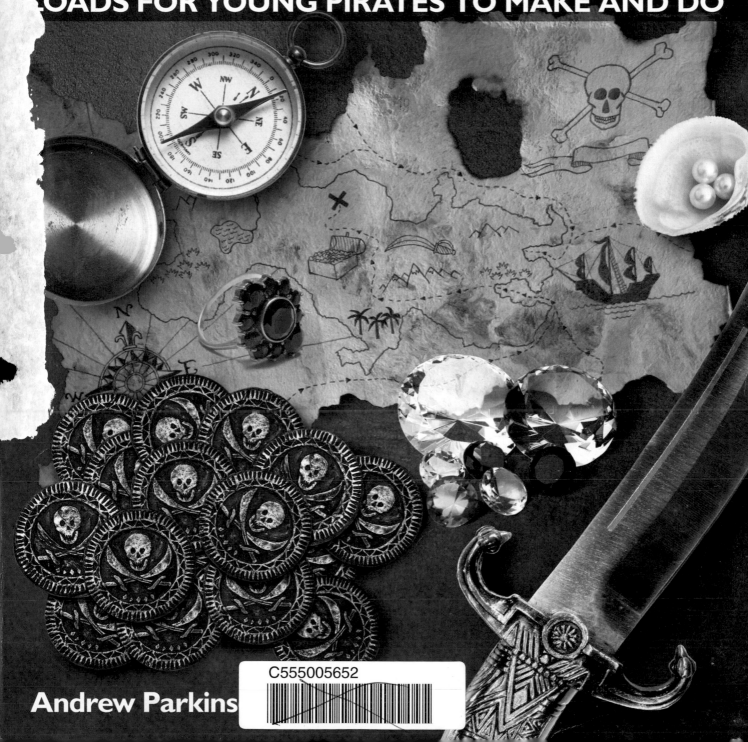

Andrew Parkins

CONTENTS

PIRATE
Manual

INTRODUCTION

EVERYTHING A YOUNG PIRATE NEEDS TO KNOW

This book aims to make you a better pirate. Maybe you've read quite a bit about pirates. Perhaps you've seen some pirate films. Or you've visited museums that have things about pirates in them. Well, now is your opportunity to learn much more – and make and do loads of things that any pirate would be proud of.

PRACTICE MAKES PERFECT PIRATES

Have you ever heard people say "practice makes perfect"? Well, this book could make you a perfect pirate in many ways.

There are many activities here. Some are easy, others a little more complicated. With all of them you'll get better with practice. Pirates had a lot of time on their hands, particularly on board ship between battles. They had plenty of time to practise things like sword skills, sewing, modelmaking, singing – everything, really! If you're twiddling your thumbs ashore at home, you can practise most of the things here.

OLDEN DAYS AND GOLDEN DAYS

Grown-ups often talk about how things were better in the olden days. Well, this book is about the golden days, when things were better for pirates.

The best time to be a pirate was probably between 1660 and 1730. This was called the golden age of piracy. There were huge fortunes floating across the seas, on great ships just waiting to be captured! Some of the most famous pirates ever lived around this time. Their pirate ships were some of the best ever, so beautiful and fast – and greatly feared.

In this book, you'll learn a lot and become well prepared to be a pirate from the golden days. That was about 300 years ago – when your dad's grandfather's great-grandfather's great-great-grandfather would have been going to school! Except – unless he was rich – he probably didn't have a chance to go to school. If he was more than 10 years old, he probably had to go to work. And it's just possible he went to sea. Do you think he become a pirate too?

WATCH OUT!

DIFFICULT TO DO?

On each project, you'll see these marks. They show how difficult each project is, from one mark for fairly easy and quick, to five marks for hardest and longest.

DIFFICULTY RATING:

ADULT HELP?

You may find that you need a little help for some of these projects – especially the ones marked with this sign.

ADULT HELP NEEDED

CUTTING OUT?

Turn to the back of the manual to find the detailed instructions for cutting out the paper or card you'll need to make some of the projects.

SEE CUTTING DIAGRAM ON PAGE 94

PIRATES AND PIRACY

Pirates come in many shapes and sizes, just like their ships! But one thing they nearly always have in common is this: they're mean and nasty, and they steal from people. And everyone finds pirates interesting!

PIRATES IN ONE PARAGRAPH

There have been all sorts of pirates over the years. They have been robbing ships for hundreds, even thousands, of years. The ancient Greeks, the Romans, the Vikings, the Crusaders all had their fair share of pirates. But being a pirate really became big business in the 16th century! Lots more ships started to carry valuable things – treasure, precious cloth and spices – all around the world. And this meant that there were more opportunities for sailors who were happy to be robbers on the high seas!

BARBARY PIRATES

If you gave pirates a score for nastiness, most of them would get 9 out of 10. But people who knew Barbary pirates would say that they deserved 12 out of 10! They operated off the Barbary Coast in North Africa for centuries, and caught hundreds of English ships. They usually used sailing ships called galleys, which had oars pulled by slaves.

CORSAIRS

After the Barbary pirates had been improving their act for a few hundred years, some of the pirates in the area started calling themselves corsairs. A corsair is the name for a fast type of sailing ship that they liked. The corsairs still captured people for slaves or ransoms (sums of money for releasing prisoners), but they also got a lot more adventurous. The most famous of the corsairs were the Barbarossa (it means 'red beard') brothers. They didn't just attack ships – they even attacked large towns.

BUCCANEERS

In the 17th and 18th centuries, some pirates were called buccaneers. The name 'buccaneer' came from the local word for barbecues in the Caribbean. These weren't just barbecues with sausages or burgers, though. They were massive. Do you fancy roasting whole cows and pigs over enormous open fires as big as your bedroom!

FREEBOOTERS

Some pirates were called freebooters. No one is quite sure why they got this name, but it may be because they got booty (things taken by force or stolen) free, or because they sometimes used fast sailing ships called flyboats (in Dutch the name sounds like 'fleeboots'!).

PIRATES

PRIVATEERS: LICENSED TO KILL . . .

A privateer was a kind of pirate with permission. He would have a special licence (called a 'letter of marque') from his government. This allowed him to capture enemy ships. However, he did have to share what he took from these ships with the government.

Sir Francis Drake was a famous privateer who made a fortune. He went to sea when he was only 14 years old. He was very successful and daring, and a brilliant leader. In 1577, he went to the Pacific Ocean and captured a Spanish treasure ship that was carrying what is equivalent to over £10 million in today's money. Not bad for a day's work! It took him three years to get home, where he built a lovely mansion and enjoyed a nice life. The queen of England, Elizabeth, was very pleased with him. She called him her very own pirate.

THE GOLDEN AGE OF PIRACY

Some people call the period between 1650 and 1730 the 'Golden Age of Piracy'. Normally we talk of a golden age being a nice time. It was good for pirates, but it wasn't for other sailors, merchants or other travellers!

If you were a pirate, you usually got caught in the end. It became very dangerous because every government was out to get you.

Anyone who had been a leading pirate could expect a horrible execution. Most died a nasty death – perhaps as nasty as the deaths they gave their victims!

CONTENTS

FAMOUS PIRATES

There were thousands of pirates, but only a few became famous. They became celebrities in the newspapers and people wrote books about them.

MOST FAMOUS?
BLACKBEARD 1680–1718

Blackbeard's real name was Edward Teach. He was probably from Bristol, which is where many sailors set out from to make their fortune. Between 1717 and 1718, Blackbeard hit the headlines for more and more fierce attacks on ships and ports. In the end he had over 400 men on six ships. He even captured other pirates' ships.

Blackbeard terrified both his friends and enemies. He wanted people to think he was a monster from hell. He had a long, black beard and used to put black ribbons in it. He also stuck lighted fuses into his hat, so there was smoke all around him!

Black Bart was a real Pirate of the Caribbean and inspiration for Jack Sparrow in the films.

This is Blackbeard. His strange looks put fear into the bravest sailors

MOST CAPTURES?
BLACK BART BARTHOLOMEW ROBERTS 1682–1722

Welshman Black Bart began life as a law-abiding sailor. In 1719, his ship was captured by pirates and he was persuaded (probably with a cutlass at his throat!) to join them. Then his career took off. In a short while he was leading a very brave crew in his ship, the *Royal Rover*. In a few years he captured about 400 ships, which is an amazing achievement!

MOST CRUEL?
TWO OF THE WORST ...

Francois L'Ollonais was a French buccaneer. He was so scary that people preferred to fight to the death than end up his prisoner. Why? He tore out people's tongues if they didn't immediately tell him where the valuables were. He would torture people and cut them to pieces. Horrible! And it's exactly what happened to him in the end, when he was captured by native Indians in South America.

PIRATE
Manual

Edward Low was one of the cruellest English pirates ever – and that's saying something! Apparently, he once cut off a man's lips and fried them in front of him. Another time he cut off a man's ears and made him eat them. Urrggh!

MOST ADVENTUROUS?
SIR HENRY MORGAN 1635–1688
Henry Morgan was Welsh, and one of the most successful buccaneers ever. He didn't just attack ships. He was a great adventurer, and also led men overland in dangerous expeditions. He once took a small army through jungle where they ran out of food and had to eat their leather luggage.

MOST UNLUCKY?
BLACK SAM BELLAMY
Black Sam Bellamy was one of the most successful pirates, but in the end he was really unlucky. His most valuable catch was in 1717 near the Bahamas islands – a slave ship called the *Whydah*. It turned out to be full of gold, silver, ivory and spices. Black Sam became a multi-millionaire overnight, so he decided it was time for him to retire. He set off to a safe spot that was a few weeks' sailing away. Unfortunately, his ship hit a storm, and he and his crew were all lost at sea.

Francois l'Ollonais - the kind of pirate to avoid if you want to stay in one piece!

DID YOU KNOW?

DARK TIMES AND BLACK GOLD

'Black gold' was a name used to refer to slaves. The golden days were horrible times for the many thousands of men, women and children who were captured in Africa. They were sold to European traders, who took them by ship in awful conditions to the Caribbean and America. Pirates sometimes seized the slaving ships and then simply sold the 'cargo' (the people on board). As you would expect, pirates did not care about it. Sadly, nor did (nearly) everyone else. People thought the slave trade was OK.

MAKE A NAME FOR YOURSELF

A pirate needs a special name. This name could grow out of your real name. Here are some different ways you can invent pirate names for yourself and your crew . . .

ALLITERATION

Alliteration is when two or more words start with the same sound. It's great using alliteration for pirate names because you end up with names like Peg-leg Pete, Silent Sal or Dangerous Dan.

You can also look out for words that share other letters, as these often sound good, as well. How about Nasty Eleanor or Hissy Chris, for example?

OPPOSITES

Some nicknames describe someone. Others make a joke by saying the opposite of what someone's like. (The most famous example is probably Robin Hood's large friend Little John.) They can be quite funny... for example, Silent Sam may really be a complete chatterbox, Big Ben may be the shortest person in the crew or Rough Rob could be a real softie...

Question

WHY DID THE CREW REFUSE TO SAY, 'AYE AYE, CAPTAIN'?

Answer

BECAUSE HE'D ONLY GOT ONE EYE!

'WHERE D'YE HAIL FROM?'

This is a piratey way of asking, 'Where do you come from?' In the golden days of piracy, many people didn't have normal surnames. Instead, they used names that showed where they lived. You can give yourself a special name that says where you're from, such as Amy Oxford, Josh London or Ellie Edinburgh. You could add your home town to your pirate name to make it longer – for example, Dangerous Debbie Devon, Long Luke Liverpool and Brave Jack Birmingham.

WHAT YOU'RE LIKE

Some nicknames describe what you're like or how you behave (or, if you're doing opposites, what you're *not* like and how you *don't* behave) – for example, Blue-eyed Brendan, Tom Crazy, Four Helpings Harry, Evil Emily or Fearless Anil.

WHAT YOU'VE GOT

Some nicknames describe your physical features or your special skills. So be extra careful around Nick the Knife, Cutthroat Christina, Tim Terrible, Axes Abbie or Chris the Cutlass!

DIFFERENT SORTS OF BOOTY

Pirates, privateers, buccaneers, corsairs – they were all after the same thing. Booty. Valuable things. Treasure. Cargo. Anything you could sell for a lot of money. This included:

GOLD AND SILVER

Have you ever noticed a security van outside a bank, or seen someone with a helmet on, collecting or delivering some money? Well, in the time of the privateers and pirates, they didn't have security vans or police guards! Lots of valuable stuff went on ships carrying heavy loads of gold and silver between countries. They sometimes had armed ships to protect the treasure, but not always. And everyone was absolutely terrified of pirates, so sometimes ships gave in without putting up a fight!

JEWELS

Pirates weren't looking for the kind of jewellery you can see in your high street! They stole highly valuable diamonds, pearls, other gems and precious stones from far-away countries… by the bucketful!

PRECIOUS GOODS

Trading ships carried spices, silks and porcelain, which were all immensely valuable in the golden days. It may seem funny today, but in the golden days a porcelain dinner plate could be worth more than £200! And if you had a sack with a few kilograms of cinnamon, nutmeg or tea to sell, your family could buy a house with it!

PEOPLE

For hundreds of years laws allowed slavery. Thousands and thousands of people were captured in Africa, and were put on ships that had dreadful living conditions. You might think normal people would take pity on them, but you would be wrong. You would probably expect pirates not to care, too. And you'd be right. Usually they simply kept them as slaves and sold them to a slave trader. But if pirates captured a ship with slaves on board, sometimes they might offer them a chance to join the crew.

Pirates also sometimes took free people and sold them into slavery. If they found an important person on board, they would fetch even more money. They would also demand money (a ransom) for their safe return – the amount of money was often huge.

MAKING MONEY

DIFFICULTY RATING:

These days, coins aren't usually made of valuable metal. But in the golden days there used to be all sorts of gold and silver coins.

Coins often had exotic names, such as Escudo (which means 'shield') or Silver Louis (lots of French kings were called Louis). But the most famous pirate coins of all were the 'pieces of eight'. This was the nickname for Spanish silver dollars, or *pesos* ('pieces'). These were worth eight *reales* ('royals') and were about the size of today's £2 coin. Other favourite coins were doubloons, which were worth twice as much as pieces of eight.

YE WILL NEED

- Pile of 2p pieces
- Thin gold and silver wrapping paper or card
- White paper
- Pencils
- Fine ballpoint pen
- Newspaper
- Scissors
- Glue stick

PIRATE
Manual

1 Place at least ten sheets of newspaper on your work surface. With the shiny side of the gold or silver paper down on the newspaper, draw around a 2p coin with a fine ballpoint pen.

2 Take a look at the coin designs here and draw your own. Press hard on your pen. Cut out the circles.

3 Put plenty of glue on the coins.

4 Stick your designs on the coins (on one or both sides).

Note: if you haven't got thin gold or silver paper, you can make your own. Just draw some squares on paper, then colour them with gold or silver pen. Let the ink dry – then follow the steps shown.

DID YOU KNOW?

GIMME A TASTE OF YOUR MONEY!

Pirates used to bite their money! Not to taste it, but to test it. Biting on a gold coin was a normal thing to do, because gold is softer than many other metals. Higher grade gold is softer still. By looking at the dent your teeth make in the coin, you can check if it's gold and find out its quality. (You could try this with a gold ring or necklace at home, but you probably won't be popular!)

PIRATE FLAGS

DIFFICULTY RATING:

When you make your own flags, you can include things that will scare people. For example,

- Skulls and crossbones
- Spears and swords
- Guns and cannons
- Wings and hearts
- Axes and daggers
- Hourglasses
- Skeletons
- Initials and words

YE WILL NEED

- Dowel rod (6mm diameter or more) or broomstick handle
- Pieces of cloth (black, white or red bits from old T-shirts, sheets etc., lightweight if possible.)
- Normal scissors for card, plus very sharp scissors for cloth

- Thin card
- Marker pen or soft pencil
- Needle and thread
- Glue (thick PVA or Copydex is especially good for this)
- Duct tape

MAKING FLAGS

1 Decide the size of flag you want. Cut the cloth about 5cm wider. Take one edge and fold it over about 3cm. Stitch or glue it so that there is enough space for your wooden rod to go through. Stitch or glue at the top.

2 Plan your design. Draw the shapes carefully on a piece of thin card. Cut out the shapes.

3 Draw round the card designs on the white cloth. If you want it on both sides of the flag, do a second set. Cut out the shapes.

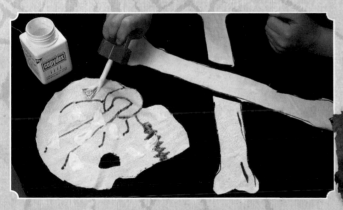

4 Glue or stitch the shapes in place on the flag. You can make finishing touches to the pieces with a black marker pen.

5 If you used glue, put the flagpole into the flag, lie the pole flat on a chair and leave the flag to dry.

6 If your flag is a bit heavy and doesn't flap enough, use duct tape to fix a dowel rod across the top at the back and on to the main handle. This will hold the flag up, and you can also take it off easily.

FAMOUS FLAGS

Everyone knows that pirates always used the black and white Jolly Roger skull and crossbones as a flag, right? No, it's wrong!

When pirates were privateers they used their country's flag, sometimes pretending to be normal trading ships. They would show their pirate flags when they got close to their victim ships – when it was too late for them to get away!

Some pirates used a plain black flag. This meant 'quarter' or mercy – they would take prisoners. However, a red flag meant 'no quarter': they would give no mercy, take no prisoners and kill everyone. The red flag was called the Jolie Rouge (French for 'pretty red'). This was really a bad joke, as the last thing you wanted to see coming towards you was a boat with a 'pretty red' flag! Eventually, Jolly Roger was a name that was given to all pirate flags.

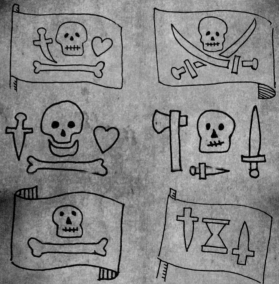

FEARSOME FLAGS

Pirates liked to show off and made up their own special flags with symbols on them to scare people! They included all sorts of things – not just skulls and crossbones, but also spears and swords, hourglasses (meaning "your time is running out"), hearts with blood coming out, initials and words.

PRECIOUS TREASURE

DIFFICULTY RATING:

Now is your chance to stash away precious things. If you don't already have lots of pieces of eight or jewels, here are some ideas.

- Rub some 1p and 2p coins with metal polish (or leave them in a jar of cola overnight – that works too!).
- Put in some chocolate coins
- Add some costume jewellery – necklaces and rings from a charity shop can be very cheap.

- Make your own treasure from small sweet cartons and other boxes. For example, paint Smartie and Toblerone tubes gold and they look just like gold ingots (bars).

YE WILL NEED

- Aluminium foil and gold and silver paper
- A4 sheet of paper
- Sellotape
- Scissors
- Pasta tubes

SILVER RINGS

1 Cut the sheet of paper in quarters. Fold a piece in half two or three times.

2 Roll the strip around your fingers and make a ring shape. Fix the ends with tape.

3 Tear off a strip of aluminium foil. To do this, press a ruler over it, and then tear the foil away carefully. Pull towards the ruler and your body, as this keeps a neat straight line.

4 Wrap the aluminium strip around the ring.

GOLD AND SILVER BARS

1 Cut small squares of gold or silver paper or foil. These need to be about 1cm wider than the pasta tubes.

2 Roll the gold or silver paper around the tubes. Tape it down if necessary.

Question

A PIRATE LOVES SOMETHING THAT HAS A HEAD AND A TAIL, BUT NO BODY. WHAT IS IT?

Answer

A COIN!

TREASURE CHEST

Every pirate needs somewhere to hide their treasure – under the bed, buried in the ground, even hidden on a desert island. Wherever you choose, having a good treasure chest is vital!

YE WILL NEED

- Shoebox
- Masking or duct tape
- Glue
- Corrugated cardboard
- Thin card (e.g., a cereal packet)
- Paints

- Paintbrushes
- Split pins (if you've got them)
- Drill with a fine drill bit, or a skewer
- Scissors or knife

SEE CUTTING DIAGRAM ON PAGE 94

PIRATE Manual

1 If the lid of your shoebox is joined to the base, that's good. If not, cut the corners at the back of the lid, so it becomes a flap. Tape this flap to the back of the box. You now have a hinged lid.

2 Draw lines on the box: four across the top, two on the front back and sides. Make them about a ruler's width apart (3-4cm).

3 Paint, following the lines, to make dark and light brown stripes.

4 Cut out all the pieces. Pieces A, B and C need to be corrugated cardboard; the rest should be thin card. Paint all of them on one side, the two A pieces black, the others gold, silver or yellow.

5 Fold piece E, and remember to cut out the holes. Glue the two middle sections together (see diagram). Cut about half a centimetre off the corners (as shown).

6 When all the paint is dry, wrap the black strips A around the box. Cut them so they go from the back of the box to the front of the lid. Glue them down, about 5cm in from each side of the box.

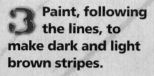

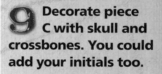

7 Do the same with the two pieces B on the bottom of the box.

8 Glue piece D in place, so that the hole for the catch is about 1cm below the edge of the lid. Glue piece C over piece D.

9 Decorate piece C with skull and crossbones. You could add your initials too.

10 Fold piece E. Then line it up with piece D and glue in place.

11 If you have some split pins, finish off by drilling holes and pushing them in to decorate the chest. The last thing to do is to make the padlock (pieces F and G in diagram). Now pour in your treasure, and hide it somewhere safe!

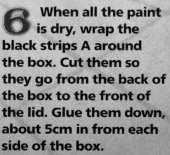

PIRATES' WEAPONS

Do you have a lot of weapons? In the golden days, a young pirate could be covered in weapons, and had lots to choose from. They always had to be ready for action! They had swords and daggers in their belts, and several pistols in an over-the-shoulder belt. Blackbeard usually had six pistols in his belt. He needed so many pistols because sometimes they wouldn't fire properly.

CANNONS

Cannons came in various sizes. The small ones were sometimes mounted on a swivel (so their direction could be changed) and were similar to modern machine-guns. Large cannons were on heavy wheeled carriages. This meant that they could be rolled back for reloading and moved for better aim.

If a cannonball landed on the deck of your ship, it would make a dent. If the cannon fired explosives, that was worse. And if you hit the powder store, that could be the end of the entire ship! But pirates usually wanted to *capture* ships, not destroy them.

Firing a cannon was a team game... It needed five or six people to do all the different jobs. Someone had to clean it, someone had to pack it with gunpowder and stuff called wadding (filler), someone had to load it with balls or shot, someone had to set the fuses, and a couple of people had to move the cannon into the right position. And one lucky person got to fire it!

FLINTLOCK PISTOLS

These worked with a type of stone called a flint. The flint made a spark when it hit against metal. This spark set off the gunpowder, which exploded in the barrel and shot out the gunshot pellets. These pistols were not very accurate, but they were deadly if you shot someone close up.

BLUNDERBUSSES

These guns had wide barrels and were very inaccurate. However, pirates liked them because they scattered shot (small bullets) and other bits of metal all over the place. You could end up with twenty little bits of metal in your body if you were in its line of fire.

MUSKETS

Muskets were much more accurate. They could hit a target at 100m. If pirates wanted to shoot someone on the deck of a ship they were approaching, a musket was the weapon to use. They could shoot both individual bullets and grapeshot. Grapeshot is the name for the small balls and bits and pieces of metal that scatter everywhere. Fired just once, it could wound and blind several people badly.

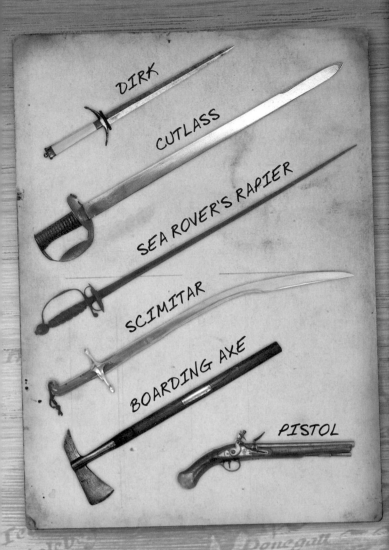

DIRK

CUTLASS

SEA ROVER'S RAPIER

SCIMITAR

BOARDING AXE

PISTOL

MISFIRE!

Pirate guns often misfired, and sometimes exploded in your face. It's one of the reasons we often think of pirates with eye patches. Historians reckon pirates were more often blinded by their own weapons than by other people's!

MAKING A STINK!

Maybe you think you know what a stink bomb is – smelly and a bit of a laugh. But they weren't so funny in the golden days. Bombs called stinkpots gave off a terrible smell, as well as smoke that left you choking and running to the side of the ship for air!

COLD STEEL

Young pirates can't rely on pistols. They're inaccurate, and reloading takes precious time. If you want to be a fiercesome fighter who never takes a break, then you'll need swords, daggers and axes like these!

CHAPTER 2

WEAPONS

CONTENTS

A SIMPLE SCIMITAR

SEE CUTTING DIAGRAM ON PAGE 95

DIFFICULTY RATING:

Some pirates had a wide-bladed scimitar. This could be very sharp, and very nasty. It's easy to make these seriously wicked swords. Luckily, they're not quite so dangerous when made out of cardboard!

YE WILL NEED

- Corrugated cardboard
- Glue
- String or cord
- scissors
- Gold and silver marker pens or paints

CARDBOARD

Did you know that corrugated cardboard is strong in one direction and weak in the other? Look carefully at a piece and you will see that it is strong along the lines and weak between them. Now try folding the cardboard lengthwise and widthwise. It's easy to fold one way, and harder to fold the other. So be careful always to cut the corrugated cardboard so that it is as strong as possible. For example, a sword blade needs the lines to follow the length of the sword.

KEEP QUIET BELOW DECKS

Imagine you are creeping up on a large ship in your smaller boat. Maybe you have crew hidden below decks, and you are going to give them a nasty surprise. (Perhaps you've seen this kind of thing in a film.) The important thing to remember is that you have to be extremely quiet. Sailing ships travel very quietly, and sounds carry over the sea. Silence is golden – it could certainly pay off, with all that treasure!

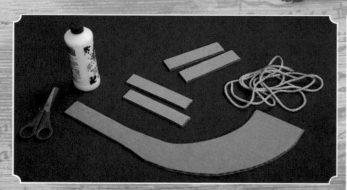

4 You can leave the handguard as it is, or cut the ends into a different shape.

1 Cut out shapes A, B and C. Try to line up the cardboard in the directions shown in the diagram. This will make your weapon much stronger. Either draw the curve of the blade (piece A) yourself or draw around a large plate.

2 To strengthen the handle, glue the handle pieces (shapes B) on either side of piece A.

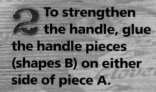

3 Glue the handguard pieces (shapes C) around the handle, as shown.

5 Tie a knot to hold the string, then wrap around the handle. Fix it with a knot or some glue. Instead of string, you could use masking or duct tape. Decorate your sword.

A PIRATE'S CUTLASS

SEE CUTTING DIAGRAM ON PAGE 95

DIFFICULTY RATING:

Successful pirates loved their cutlasses! These swords had one very sharp side, and were really good for cutting into rigging and sails. Nastier pirates found that cutlasses were great for hands and legs, too. Luckily, these days young pirates prefer to take captives in one piece!

YE WILL NEED

- Corrugated cardboard
- Ruler
- Scissors
- Glue
- Gold and silver marker pens or paint

DANGER! DANGER!

Even toy swords can be dangerous. When you're play fighting, NEVER point a sword above chest level. And keep it well away from faces and eyes. Have you seen how in some film sword fights someone holds their sword to a person's neck? DON'T try this at home, because it really can hurt.

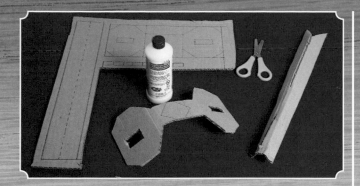

1 Mark out the pieces. Decide how long you want your sword to be – somewhere between 40cm and 60cm. Cut out the shapes. Make sure the corrugated cardboard has its lines going along piece A, as this makes it much stronger. As you will need eight identical pieces of small shape C, it's quicker to cut these from one strip of cardboard. This needs to be 15mm wide by 240mm long.

2 Piece B, the handguard, might look complicated, but it isn't really. Check the diagrams to see how to draw the right shape.

3 On piece A, draw hard with a pencil along the dotted line, and use a ruler. This pencil line makes it easier to fold.

4 Fold piece A in half lengthways. Start on the side away from the fold and cut to a point.

5 Bend the thin part of piece B around your wrist.

6 Slip each end of piece B over the top of the blade.

7 Hold the handguard in position. Glue the eight small rectangles (pieces C) on to the blade. You need to stick them on all sides of the handguard to hold it in position (see the photo on p24) Leave glue to dry, then decorate with markers or paint. Now it's time for battle!

A SEA ROVER'S RAPIER

DIFFICULTY RATING:

A rapier is great for a duel against another fearless young pirate. You can practise fancy footwork and clever fencing movements with it. As it has such a long blade, you may be able to stretch much further forward than your enemy can.

YE WILL NEED

- Old newspaper
- Large plastic fizzy drinks bottle
- Sharp knife
- Scissors
- Duct or masking tape
- Piece of thin dowel or bamboo (4–6mm diameter and 55cm long)

SWORD HOLDER

1. For most swords, and for the ring that goes on your belt, fold an A4 sheet of paper in half widthways. Fold three times more in the same direcion. For a scimitar holder, fold the A4 sheet lengthways, and the same direction twice more.

2. Now you have a strip, several layers thick. Bend it around your finger, to make a sort of flat oval ring. Put one end into the other, overlapping by about 2cm. Secure with tape.

3. Make another ring. Before you stick it together, slip it through the first ring. Decorate the holder. Fit it on to your belt and you're ready to fight…

1 Ask an adult to cut the plastic bottle in half with a knife. Then put tape around the part of the bottle that is to be cut. This will help you cut in a straight line with scissors.

5 Roll these sheets around the handle end of the sword.

2 Take ten sheets of newspaper. Lay the dowel rod along one edge, with one end about 2cm from the other edge (as in photo) and fix with tape. This will be the point of the sword. This extra bit of paper is for safety.

6 Slip the sword blade through the neck of the bottle. Tape it on the blade side (to hold it in position).

7 Cover the blade with duct tape. Cover the guard and handle with tape.

3 Roll the newspaper tightly round the dowel. Use some pieces of masking tape to hold the newspaper down.

4 Tear ten strips of newspaper 10cm wide. Hold your ruler firmly on the paper. Then pull down and towards the ruler (or cut with scissors).

Question
WHY DID CAPTAIN HOOK CROSS THE ROAD?

Answer
TO GET TO THE SECOND-HAND SHOP!

A MIDSHIPMAN'S DIRK

DIFFICULTY RATING:

A midshipman is an officer on a ship. In the golden days, many of them were also pirates. A dirk is a type of dagger. It was often a pirate's best friend because it had so many uses. In fighting, a dirk would often be held in one hand, with a sword in the other. Pirates would practise throwing it at targets. They would even go to bed with a dirk under their pillow, so they were ready for a fight!

YE WILL NEED

- Glue
- Knife or strong scissors
- Thin cardboard
- Kebab stick
- Masking tape
- 5p piece
- Paint

SEE CUTTING DIAGRAM ON PAGE 96

PIRATE
Manual

1 Having looked at the cutting diagram on page 96, carefully measure and mark all the pieces on some thin card, like a cereal packet. Cut them all out.

2 Score firmly or cut lightly into the cardboard (but not right through!). Then fold the blade (piece A) in half along this cut mark, and open out again. Carefully place the kebab stick so that it goes along the middle of one side. If necessary, cut or break it so that it is about 2cm shorter than the blade. Tape it down so that it goes right up to one end (the handle end) and is 1–2cm from the other (sharp) end.

3 Glue the blade and fold it over. You may need masking tape to hold it together (you can remove this later). Leave to dry.

4 Put a mark 8cm from the top of the handle on both edges. Make a cut about 1–1½cm in from each edge.

5 Fold the cardboard over on each side and tape it down.

6 Draw a long curve to shape the blade, then cut both edges.

7 Fold pieces B and C in half, and then half again. Open them out, and put glue along each strip. Then fold again, and fix with more glue on either side of the blade.

8 Stick pieces D and E, and F and G, on each side of the dirk. The round parts should be up on one side and down on the other. You may need masking tape to hold this part together.

9 Roll piece H round a marker pen. Let it unroll a bit, and put some glue on. Then roll it up again. Put some glue on the handle of the dirk and slip this roll over.

10 Roll piece J around a pen. Unroll it a bit, and add glue. Then stick it with more glue at the end of the handle.

11 Paint the blade and guard silver and gold. Some dirks had ivory handles, and cream paint on your dagger will look quite like ivory.

MAKING AN AXE

An axe is a great weapon for a pirate fight. You can swing it around, hack at rigging and sails, chop down a mast or two and give enemies some nasty surprises.

ADULT HELP NEEDED

YE WILL NEED

- Corrugated cardboard
- Dowel rod (18mm diameter and about 50cm long)
- Ruler
- Saw
- Scissors
- Hammer
- Nails
- glue

SEE CUTTING DIAGRAM ON PAGE 96

Question

WHAT'S A PIRATE'S FAVOURITE FOOD?

Answer

AAARRR'TICHOKES!

WORTH YOUR WEIGHT IN GOLD?

There are stories saying that pirates sometimes shared out their loot by weighing the crew and giving them their weight in gold! Do you think you're worth your weight in gold? Your mum and dad probably think so – on a good day... But what's all that gold worth? Let's say you weigh 20kg. That would make you and a couple of mates worth a million! (Of course, lots of people know you're worth much, much more than money, but unfortunately that's all pirates are interested in!)

3 When the glue has dried, wrap blade piece A around the cardboard sandwich (of B pieces) and glue together.

4 Put glue on the dowel handle and push it up into the axe head. Put a line of glue on the blade and handle, and bend piece C round.

1 Cut the dowel handle to length. Cut out the cardboard pieces, following the lines of the cardboard as in the diagram. Fold piece A in half.

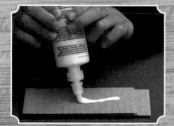 

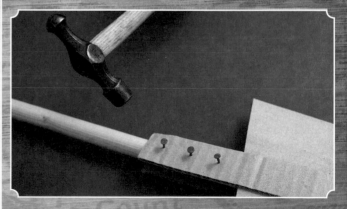

2 You're going to make a thick sandwich of the five B pieces. They don't go exactly on top of one another, but are stepped in on either side of the middle piece by about 1cm. If you are using dowel thicker than 2cm, make the axe thicker by adding two or three extra pieces of cardboard shape B. Take a look at the picture. From above, the axe head looks pointed.

5 Hammer in three nails on one side. Repeat on the other side of the blade. You may need an adult to help you with this. Paint or decorate to finish.

MAKING A CANNON

DIFFICULTY RATING

If you can learn to fire a cannon accurately, you can get a job on any pirate ship in the world! Unfortunately, real cannons are too big to use at home. This cannon allows you to practise your firing skills. It fires Maltesers, marbles and lots more. You can see how to make the cannonball rack (or brass monkey) on page 35.

ADULT HELP NEEDED

YE WILL NEED

- 5 sheets of A4 paper
- 2 dowel rods 16mm diameter (12cm long and 28–32cm long)
- 1 dowel rod 6mm diameter (4cm long)
- Thin cardboard (e.g., cereal packet), to make 9 strips 21cm x 15mm

- 2 wide elastic bands, about 6–8cm long
- Balsa wood – 25mm wide 10mm thick: 2 pieces 14cm long, 4 pieces 20cm long
- 2 dowel rods 16mm diameter, 9cm long
- 2 dowel rods 6mm diameter, 7cm long
- Thin cardboard to make 4 strips 15mm x 10cm

- Masking tape
- Drill and 6mm drill bit
- Saw or craft knife
- Drawing pins or nails
- Scissors
- Blu-Tack
- Ruler
- Pen
- Paint

SEE CUTTING DIAGRAM ON PAGE 37

MAKING THE CANNON

1 Roll the sheets of paper tightly around the long piece of dowel rod.

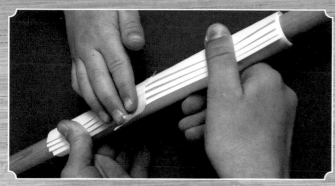

2 Tape down the sheets all along the rod. Carefully pull the tube of paper off the dowel.

3 Put some glue on the tube at the end, and along one of the cardboard strips.

4 Wrap the strip tightly around the tube.

5 Repeat this with two more strips – one for the other end and one for the middle of the tube.

6 (Ask an adult to help you with this.) For the firing rod, take the 16mm by 12cm piece of dowel, and drill a 6mm hole in the middle of one end. This is easier to do if you first drill a small hole, about 2mm in the middle. It doesn't matter if the hole isn't perfectly in the middle or straight. Put the 6mm by 4cm dowel in the hole and glue.

7 Glue one of the long strips of card around the firing rod, 4cm from the handle end.

8 This next step is tricky, and you'll need adult help. But if you don't get it right you can always take the cardboard off and start again. Put the firing rod into the gun barrel. Hook the elastic bands around the thin part of the firing rod.

9 Put some glue along another cardboard strip. Thread the strip through the elastic bands. Then wrap it next to the strip on the barrel closest to the firing rod. Leave to dry.

Your cannon is ready to fire. Pull the firing pin back carefully – but not too far! Then let go. If you put a mark on the firing pin about 15mm from the end, it will show you how far to pull and you'll avoid pulling it out. If your cannon doesn't fire far enough, try stronger elastic bands. Or, for more fire power, try fitting more bands.

MAKING THE GUN CARRIAGE

1 Ask an adult to help you to cut the balsa wood with a fine saw or craft knife.

2 Glue the six pieces as in the diagram and the next two photos.

5 Repeat all the way round with the four short strips of cardboard.

6 Fix both of the 7cm pieces of 6mm dowel under the gun barrel (see photo below) with two blobs of Blu-Tack.

3 Take the four strips of card 15mm wide x 10cm long. Roll and glue them round both ends of each of the 9cm dowel rods. Lay the rods in position on the base of the gun carriage. They will be the wheels and axles.

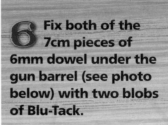

4 Take one strip of cardboard 15mm x 8cm long. Add some glue. Bend the card over the axles. Stick in drawing pins or nails.

7 The cannon can now rest on the gun carriage. You can put the second piece of 6mm dowel under the barrel now. This sets the trajectory of the gun for firing. To finish off, paint the cannon and its carriage.

FIRING A CANNON

There are three important things to get right when firing a cannon.

1. How high up or down you point. This is called the trajectory. If you change the angle of this gun, you change where the cannon fires. Easy!

2. The force – which usually means how much gunpowder you use. This cannon uses rubber bands rather than gunpowder – it's easier (and legal!) to get them in the shops. Instead of lighting a fuse, you pull back the firing rod.

3. The ammunition. You'll find that things fire differently. Try making little balls of scrunched up paper then kitchen foil – both will fly, but which will work better?

MAKING A MALTESER MONKEY

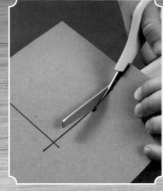

1 Mark out and cut a 85mm by 85mm square of cardboard.

2 Cut the kebab sticks to get six pieces 90–95mm long. An easy way to cut a stick is to hold it against the scissors and turn it. Then hold the kebab stick between your thumbs and snap it neatly.

3 Put a line of glue on opposite edges of the card. Press down two sticks, and put a dot of glue at each end of them.

4 Lay two more sticks across, resting them on the first sticks. Put a dot of glue at each end.

5 Lay two more sticks down in the same direction as the first two. Then leave the glue to dry.

6 Colour the brass monkey. When it is dry, pile up your cannonball Maltesers.

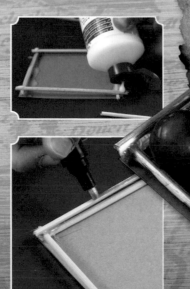

DID YOU KNOW?

BRASS MONKEYS

A brass monkey is a container for cannonballs. On board ship, pirates would stack a pile of them neatly next to their cannon, so they were ready to fire. The brass monkey you can make here will hold a neat pyramid of round things such as sweets like Maltesers, or marbles and balls of tin foil.

Sometimes people use this phrase on a really cold day: 'It's cold enough to freeze the balls off a brass monkey.' Some people think it's a bit rude. It's not! When the weather gets really cold, the rails on a brass monkey contract (get smaller), and the cannon balls can fall off!

CANNON TARGET PRACTICE

DIFFICULTY RATING:

Here's a good target for firing practice with the cannon on page 32. Test your own firing skills, or compete against someone else, and become a master gunner. Score 10 points for hitting the main mast sails, 5 points for the other masts. If the 'ball' lands in the ship, score 2 points. Give each gunner four shots in each round.

YE WILL NEED

- 2 A4 sheets of paper
- 3 kebab sticks or other thin sticks
- 3 bottle tops – cork (preferably) or plastic (from fizzy drinks bottles)
- Large baking tin
- Scissors
- Marker pens

Question

WHY DO PIRATES WEAR HATS WHEN FIGHTING?

Answer

THEY NEED SOMEWHERE TO KEEP THEIR HEADS IN BATTLE!

1 Fold the A4 paper in four and open out again. Cut in four along the creases (as shown).

2 Fold and cut one rectangle in half, to make two smaller rectangular sails.

3 Fold and cut one of the larger rectangles in half diagonally. This makes two triangular sails.

4 Push the kebab sticks into each of the three bottle tops. If you are using plastic caps, ask an adult to make a small hole in the middle with a drill or hot nail.

5 Fold each paper sail in half. Make a small snip at the top and bottom, on the fold to create holes for the masts to fit through. For the triangular sail, make a fold about 1cm in from the upright edge. Then snip across the fold.

6 Cut out a small rectangle for the flag and decorate it. You can make more flags for the other masts. Cut these flags like you did for the sails. Slip the sails and flags over the kebab sticks.

7 Stand the masts carefully in the roasting tin. They should be ready to topple over if a cannonball hits them. If they are too wobbly, use a blob of Blu-Tack to steady them.

EDIBLE CANNONBALLS

Here are some of the things we've tried and fired well: Maltesers, Cadbury's Shots, hard-boiled sweets, marbles, small stones, aluminium foil scrunched up into small balls, pen lids and mint imperials (which fire brilliantly!).

Be very careful about firing indoors. Ask an adult to help you decide how, where and what you can fire. Never aim at anyone's face – even a sweet can cause an injury!

LET'S GET DRESSED

Shiver me timbers! Here be wicked clothes to make thee look real good and real bad, too. Ye'll soon be the perfect picture of a pretty pirate. . . Aaarr!

KEEP YOUR HAIR OUT
Tie some cloth around your head to keep your hair back. Pirates often had long hair.

NO TIME TO WASH!
Because of the gunpowder and greasy equipment pirates usually have a grubby face and hands. Don't worry about washing more than once a week! Captain's orders!

JEWELLERY
You might be allowed one earring, but not chains or other jewellery. They just get in the way when you're fighting.

TOPS
If you want long sleeves, tie them up so they won't catch on anything. Otherwise, cut the sleeves to the elbow.

HAVING A SLASHING TIME?
After a hard day's fighting, you might find that your top has got a bit tattered. Make some cuts on the arms and the front and back.

PROTECT YOURSELF
Wrap cloths round your wrists and neck. If some masts are hit, or cannonballs and shot are flying around, you'll want a bit of protection here.

DAGGER FOR A DAY'S WORK
You'd need a dagger for your work every day – cutting ropes, wood, food etc. Handy for battle too!

TROUSERS
These mustn't flap around too much. Cut them just below the knee.

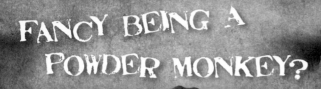

FANCY BEING A POWDER MONKEY?

Are you under 16? Then pirates would expect you to be a powder monkey! This was quite a tough job. Powder monkeys had to bring bullets for the officers, gunpowder and shot for the gun crews, wood for the cook's stoves and sometimes even acted as waiter at dinner!

CHAPTER 3

LOOKING BAD

CONTENTS

AN EYE PATCH

In just a few minutes, you can make yourself an eye patch and instantly terrify the family!

YE WILL NEED

- Some thin cardboard (e.g., from a cereal packet)
- Pen
- Scissors
- Masking tape, Sellotape or glue
- Black paint
- Black or white elastic (50–60cm for each patch)

PIRATE EARRINGS

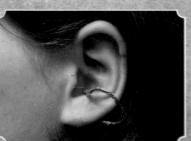

1 Get a small paperclip, some gold or coloured paper, ruler, pencil, scissors and sellotape. With the pencil and ruler, mark out and cut a thin strip of coloured paper about 3mm wide by 12cm long.

2 Straighten out the paperclip. With a small piece of tape, fix the paper at one end of the straightened paperclip. Cover the whole clip in paper by wrapping round. (Tip: It may be easier to turn the clip and let the paper get pulled on to it, rather than trying to wrap the paper round the clip.)

3 Bend the wire around your fingers or a thick marker pen. You need to end up with a circular ring. Then hook the earring above your earlobe.

1. **Draw an oval shape, about 6cm wide and 5cm high. Then cut it out. You might need to try a few different sizes to get the right one for you and your fellow pirates.**

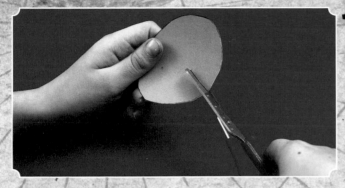

2. **Cut a short slit (about 2cm) in the top. Pull the card to get it to overlap at the slit. Hold down with tape or glue.**

3. **With the point of your scissors, make small holes on either side of the patch.**

4. **Measure the elastic around your pirate's head, and cut it to the right length (it needs to be stretched a little bit). Thread the elastic through the holes, with the elastic running across the back. Knot the two ends together to make a single loop to go over your head.**

5. **Finish off by painting the eye patch black. Then get ready to scare the neighbours (or the cat)!**

DID YOU KNOW?

LOSING AN EYE

If a pirate lost an eye, it often meant that he would soon lose his life, as well. You're never so good at fighting when you can only see with one eye. This is because it is harder to judge distances. Try reaching out for things with your patch on. Check out your swordplay. Does it feel different? Are you better or worse when you're using just one eye?

Question

HOW MUCH DID THE PIRATE PAY FOR HIS EARRINGS?

Answer

A BUCK-AN-EAR!

A HORRIBLE HOOK

Sometimes pirates had hooks, if their hands had been wounded. Pirates and sailors often had amputations (limbs removed) to avoid infections that could kill. They didn't have anaesthetics (medicine we have today to take away pain). Their hands, arms and legs were just sawn off. Aaarrgh! This hook is horrible, but luckily the only thing that has to be cut off is the top of a drinks bottle!

ADULT HELP NEEDED

YE WILL NEED

- Large plastic drinks bottle, without lid
- Masking or duct tape
- Coat hanger with wire hook
- Paint or markers

1 Ask an adult to pull the wire hook out of a plastic coat hanger (or to cut the hook off an all-wire coat hanger).

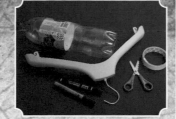

4 Push the hook through the bottle lid. Then wrap more tape over the bottle so that the hook doesn't wobble too much.

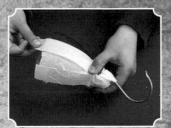

2 Get an adult to cut the drinks bottle in half with a sharp knife. You can then easily cut it smaller with scissors. Cut to a size that fits your hand.

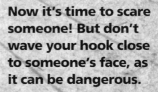

5 Wrap more tape around the straight section inside, to make a comfortable handle. Cover the outside with masking tape. Use marker pens or paint to make it black and gold.

Now it's time to scare someone! But don't wave your hook close to someone's face, as it can be dangerous.

3 Wrap several layers of tape around the straight bit of the hook.

HORRIBLE THREATS

Pirates made terrible threats to their enemies and prisoners. And unfortunately they often carried them out. Today's young pirates don't want to be so horrid to their victims, though. Maybe you'd just like to remember these threats and use them only with friends! These are some of the nicer things pirates would say…

ANYONE FOR TARGET PRACTICE?

I'LL SLICE YOU LIKE A LOAF OF BREAD

HOW MANY BITS WOULD YOU LIKE TO BE IN?

BONES IS WHAT YOU'LL BE…

I'LL BLAT YOU OVER THE HORIZON

I'LL INTRODUCE YOU TO THE SHARKS

A CAPTAIN'S PARROT

DIFFICULTY RATING: ⚔ ⚔ ⚔ ⚔ ⚔

Pirates and parrots go together like fish and chips. In the golden days pirates would teach their parrots to say terrible things. This paper parrot doesn't say much, but it will look very cool on your shoulder or perching on an armchair!

ADULT HELP NEEDED

YE WILL NEED

- Coloured paper (Parrots are all sorts of colours. We used yellow, red, blue, white and black paper. What will you choose?)
- Toilet-roll tube
- Sellotape
- Glue

- 4 medium-sized safety pins
- Scissors
- Ruler
- Marker pens
- Blu-Tack

SEE CUTTING DIAGRAM ON PAGE 98

7 Fold piece G in half. Then bend and tape it over the beak and on to the body, on both sides.

1 Cut out all the pieces. Draw two spirals on shapes H and J and two thick lines on piece F.

2 Roll piece A around the toilet roll tube. Then tape it. Its narrower side makes the height of the body.

8 Put a dot of glue on the head and stick down the two eyes (H and J).

9 Tape or glue piece K (the legs) into the bottom of the tube at the front.

3 Bend round and tape or glue pieces B and C at the back of the tube. This makes the tail.

10 For piece L, use a whole A4 sheet. Fold it in half lengthways, then again and again so you have a folded strip about 5cm x 30cm. Tape it to hold it together. Put safety pins at each end around the strip about 5cm apart and tape them in place.

11 Bend the strip, and push it into the base by about 2–4cm. Then tape it to the base on both sides.

4 Bend round, then tape or glue pieces D and E at the sides of the tube. These form wings.

5 Make a 1cm cut in the parrot's body at the top in the front. Make a similar cut on piece F (the beak).

12 To make your parrot look more feathery, make short snips into the head at the back, the wings and the tail. Are you ready to perch him somewhere? Just attach the safety pins to keep the parrot still on your shoulder or armchair.

6 Push piece F on to the top of the body. The two cuts need to fit into one another.

BELTS AND BUCKLES

Pirates liked to steal fancy clothes from their prisoners but you can buy clothes, belts and buckles cheaply from a charity shop. You can also make some yourself: A fine pirate needs a good strong belt round the waist. And another one around the shoulder!

YE WILL NEED

- Webbing or other strip of material
- 5 lolly sticks
- Craft knife
- Pen, paper and set square
- wood glue
- Gold or silver paint or marker pens

Question

WHY DOES IT TAKE PIRATES SO LONG TO LEARN THE ALPHABET?

Answer

BECAUSE THEY CAN SPEND YEARS AT C!

You can use all sorts of material to make your pirate belt. Upholstery webbing is really useful. You can cut it to the right size and fit it over your shoulder. It is sold in good department stores, craft shops and DIY shops. Calico or canvas are also good belt materials. You can cut it in long strips. And, if you're good at sewing, you can turn over the edges and stitch it. This will make it even smarter. You can also simply tear a strip from an old sheet, roll it over two or three times and make a kind of belt that way.

1 Draw a guide for the buckle on some paper.

2 Cut your lolly sticks. Place two of the longer pieces on the guide. Put two dots of glue on each end and stick down the two shorter pieces. Glue the sticks together.

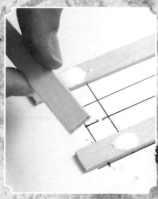

3 Glue the last piece on top of the others, and then leave to dry.

4 Paint your buckle gold or silver. To fix the belt over your shoulder or round your waist, thread one end through the buckle first, then the other.

PIRATE TALK

Pirates tend to talk in a strange way. They often have several different ways of saying the same thing. If in doubt, just add 'Aaarr' to a normal sentence. Pirates use hundreds of words and phrases, and here are some really useful ones.

AYE, AAARR! . . . . Yes

NAY . . . . No

HA (HAARR!) . . . . Yeah, right

AHOY THERE . . . . Hello

BY YOUR LEAVE . . . . Please

I THANK THEE TRULY . . . . Thank you

GOOD MORROW . . . . Good morning

FARE YE WELL .Goodbye

'OW'S IT WITH YE? . . . . .How are you doing?

'OO BE THEE THEN? . . . . Who are you?

TERRIBLE TIM IS ME. . . . . . . .My name is Tim

AFT THERE! . . . . .Hey, you in the back!

B'LOW THERE! . . . . Hey you downstairs!

FOR'ARD THERE! . . . . . .Hey you at the front!

BEND YER EAR TO THIS . . . Everyone, listen

GET ALONG LIVELY! . . . . Hurry up!

SHAKE YER TIMBERS! . . . . Get up!

JUMP LIVELY .Let's go

OPEN YER LUGHOLES! . . . . .Listen!

DROP ANCHOR . . . . .Stop

BRING UP ALONGSIDE . . . . Come here

PIRATE'S HAT

DIFFICULTY RATING:

With this on your head, you'll be able to take command of any pirate ship!

YE WILL NEED

- Cardboard from a whole large cereal packet (ideally 29cm tall)
- Pen
- Scissors
- Masking tape
- Yellow or white paper
- Black paint
- Bowl or plate

SEE CUTTING DIAGRAM ON PAGE 99

TOMBSTONE HAT

1 You will need one A3 sheet of black card (or thin card like we've used, painted black) Follow the diagram. Cut off a 2cm strip. Then score the dotted lines (this means you make a line in the card with scissors or pressing hard with a ballpoint pen, to make folding easier). Using a bowl measuring about 20cm, mark a semicircle on the sheet. Cut around the semicircle.

2 Score the sheet. Then fold it in half. Make sure the semicircle is sticking upwards.

3 Decorate your hat – cut out shapes in paper and stick them on the hat. You can also put paint on your design.

4 Add three pieces of tape on either side. Shape the hat, using the folds where you scored lines in steps 1 and 2.

SEE CUTTING DIAGRAM ON PAGE 99

1 Open up the cereal box carefully. Cut along one edge so that most of it can still be used. Draw the pattern on the cardboard. Make sure that the folds from the cereal packet are kept in the middle (as shown).

2 Find a plate or bowl that measures about the same as your head. Mark a circle on some scrap paper. Then cut it out, to check it's the right size. When you have found the correct size, mark the circle on the cardboard. Make sure it is the same distance from the left and right diagonal lines (about 1–2cm away).

3 Cut out the shape. Score along the dotted lines (this means you make a line in the card with scissors or by pressing hard with a ballpoint pen, to make folding it easier).

5 Paint the hat black. Cut out about twenty squares in yellow or white paper. These should measure 3cm by 3cm. Then fold the squares in half to make triangles.

4 Fold the two side pieces upwards. If necessary, stick a piece of masking tape at the front. This will hold them together.

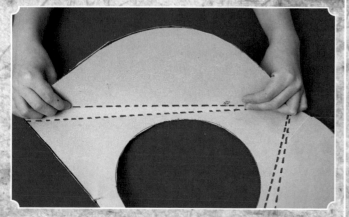

6 Glue the triangles on to the edge of the hat. Cut and glue more squares if you need them.

THE PIRATE SHIP

Jump lively! Weigh anchor! Ready to set sail, me hearties! We'll soon see thee a master mariner and a perfect pirate, too. We'll make thee feel at home when yer at sea!

DIFFERENT TYPES OF PIRATE SHIP

Pirates liked fast ships that could out run and move fast around larger trading ships. They often sailed quite small boats, carrying maybe only ten pirates. But trading ships were often hardly armed and the Jolly Roger was enough to strike such fear in to their victims to surrender immediately.

Some pirates also captured and used larger ships, even the largest warships.

Some ships had oars as well as sails for extra speed

A warship was a very fast fighting machine, with a crew of over 200 and more than 50 cannons

A PIRATE SHIP NEEDS TO BE:

FAST
You need to be able to catch up with your enemies, and overtake them! By unfurling (undoing) the correct sails quickly and catching the wind right, the ship accelerates (speeds up) quickly.

VERY MANOEUVRABLE
You need to be able to get past your victims, get around them and cut them off, so they cannot move any further. If you have an experienced captain, a pirate ship can have a smaller turning circle compared with other ships. By reducing sails (making the sails smaller) and dropping special anchors, the ship slows down fast.

WELL ARMED
You need enough cannons to scare your victims. About twelve cannons are enough, because you can wheel them all over to one side.

WELL MANNED
You need enough crew for a good fight. A large cannon needs a team of five or six to keep it going, so that's quite a lot to start with!

CHAPTER 4

ALL ABOARD

JOBS ON A PIRATE SHIP

BOSUN (BOATSWAIN)
He was in charge of keeping things neat and tidy on board, especially the ship's sails and rigging.

QUARTERMASTER
He was second in command. He was also in charge of the loot (valuables) taken on board. He had to keep them safe and make sure they were shared out fairly.

NAVIGATOR
He was responsible for planning the routes. You had to be very good at maths and geometry for this job!

GUNNER
He supervised all the cannon crews.

COOK
What did he do? Yes, he cooked, but he had another job… doctor! If there wasn't a trained doctor on board, the cook would do the amputations – which means cutting hands, arms and legs off to avoid diseases. Urrggh!

CAPTAIN
That was a nice job, bossing everyone around! But you had to watch out! Your crew might have got fed up with you – and left you marooned on land or thrown you overboard!

POWDER MONKEY
This was a good start to your career. You'd fetch and carry for the gun crew and officers, getting to know everything going on above and below deck.

CONTENTS

BLACKBEARD'S PIRATE SHIP

This drawing shows The Queen Anne's Revenge, Blackbeard's flagship. He used it to lead a fleet of six ships. In 1718 they captured 9 ships in one week!

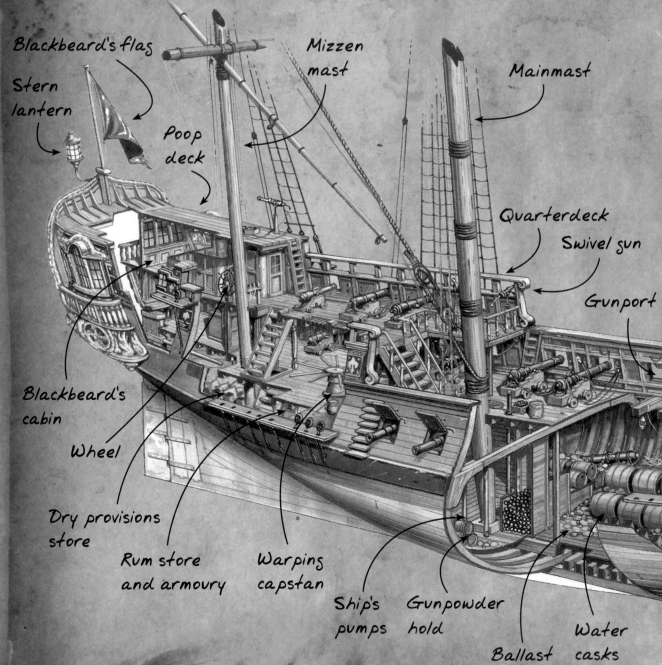

Blackbeard's flag

Stern lantern

Mizzen mast

Mainmast

Poop deck

Quarterdeck

Swivel gun

Gunport

Blackbeard's cabin

Wheel

Dry provisions store

Rum store and armoury

Warping capstan

Ship's pumps

Gunpowder hold

Ballast

Water casks

PORT OR STARBOARD?

It's essential for a pirate to know his port and starboard, just as landlubbers need to know their left from right. Standing on deck, looking towards the bow (front) of a ship – the left side is called the port side and the right is called the starboard side.

Foremast

Rigging

Spritsail topmast

Heads

Bowsprit

Capstan

Position of figurehead (lost in storm before vessel was captured)

Anchor

Crew's quarters

THE QUEEN ANN'S REVENGE

Length	110ft (34m)
Armament	40 guns
Pirate crew	up to 300men

PARTS OF A PIRATE SHIP

You'd soon get used to knowing where everything is aboard ship, and what it's all called. Read on here and see how much you can find in the picture of Blackbeard's ship on the previous page...

CAPSTAN
'Weigh anchor' means 'lift the anchor'. You wind up the anchor with the capstan, which is shaped like a merry-go-round. But it's no plaything. Up to eight strong pirates may be needed to push this around!

ANCHOR
Most people know that anchors hold a ship still. Pirates also know how to use them to slow down when sailing and attacking

SWIVEL GUNS
Ready, aim, fire! These guns look a bit like modern machine-guns, and you can aim them quickly. But you couldn't fire more than twenty shots per hour! That's one every 3 minutes.

CROW'S NEST
Climb up here and on a clear day you can see for 30km. Don't fall asleep on watch here. Two reasons: 1) you could fall off, and 2) some pirates punish the watchman with death if he falls asleep on watch. This is not surprising, really, because everyone's life depended on the person on watch. Their job is to look out for danger.

MAN THE PUMPS!
Ships usually take on extra water from leaks and from waves splashing over the decks. Most of it ends up in the bilges, dirty, smelly tanks deep below deck. Pirates need to be ready to pump water out – to keep the ship as light as possible.

BALLAST
This is rubble (heavy stones) to keep the boat balanced. However, if you have treasure on board, throw some ballast off the ship to make space for it!

SAILS
Are you good at sewing? Keeping the sails in good shape is an important job. There might be a spare set, but as soon as a sail is damaged, quick repair is vital to keep the ship sailing at top speed.

GUNPOWER HOLD
Often with specially protected walls, gunpowder is kept here, deep down in the ship, out of the way – and safe (you hope!)

GALLEY
Dinner time? This is where the cooking is done.

FOOD HOLD
Food is kept safely away from rats, weevils and mould? No chance!

ARMOURY (ARSENAL)
This is where weapons are stored.

SHIP'S WHEEL
Are you strong? You need to be to turn the ship's wheel, especially in bad weather! It moves the rudder to change the ship's direction. The helmsman works the wheel, and takes orders from the captain or another officer.

PIRATE
Manual

FIGUREHEAD

Some ships had an impressive wooden carving to decorate the front of the ship. They were usually of curvy ladies.

TENDERS AND LONGBOATS

You can't take a large ship into shallow water, so you need small boats to take you and your crew onto beaches and into towns. A tender is the name for a small boat that is often pulled along behind a larger ship. Don't expect lifeboats on board – longboats can take some of the crew – but not all – if the ships sinks.

CATCH MORE WIND!

Sails sometimes have to be tied up (*furled*) and untied (*unfurled*) quickly. You open up the sails to catch more wind and speed, and furl them to slow down. If you get it wrong, you'll find yourself whizzing past a treasure ship and not be able to turn around quickly!

RIGGING

Rigging is the name for all the ropes for the masts and sails. Some of it is like a rope climbing frame, making it quite easy to climb fast. A team of sailors would be able to reach and furl or unfurl the sails in a few minutes.

HEAD TO THE TOILET

Some ships have proper toilets – or, rather, wooden seats with holes, placed right over the sea! Others don't, so if you had to go to the loo you did it at the 'heads', which is a bit like doing it over a climbing frame!

ROPES KEPT NEATLY

A well-run pirate ship needs hundreds of metres of rope, which must be kept neat and tidy. This means it is instantly ready for use and no one's going to trip up over it in the middle of a fight.

GET YOUR DRINK HERE!

The rum store needs strong locks. After a successful day, your crew might be allowed a few drinks. They usually can't wait !

WHAT'S THE TIME?

Someone is in charge of keeping the time. It's a bit like the school bell ringing to tell you it's dinnertime. They check the hourglass, and when the sand runs out it's time to ring the bell.

DID YOU KNOW?

RATS RUNNING RIOT!

Rats were a real problem on a ship – and they still can be today (although people who run luxury liners don't want to admit this!). They eat your stores, they nibble at things and they will even bite you. Also, they breed fast. In the golden days, ships often had more rats than pi-rats!

CAPTURING A SHIP

How do you capture a ship? It's easy when you're a clever captain. Make sure you have a good ruthless pirate crew on board, and just follow these simple steps...

SHIP AHOY!
Using your lookouts and telescope, do some homework. Check out the size and quality of the ship's crew. Do they look good? How fast is their ship? Is she a good one? Can she turn quickly?

TRUST US, WE'RE SAILORS!
Pirates pretend to be normal sailors. They fly false flags. This means they show normal flags, like the English St George cross, to make them *seem* safe.

HIDE THE CANNONS!
Covering cannons and gunports (openings in the ship's side) with netting and canvas will make people think your ship is not armed.

BOARDING CREW, HIDE!
Hide your crew and weapons. Put them below deck, or cover them up with boxes. Make it look like your ship is an innocent trading vessel.

PLAY YOUR PARTS!
Make everything look safe and harmless. Dress up some of your crew as women! Pretend that everyone is busy with normal activities, playing cards, preparing dinner, etc.

STEADY AHEAD!
Get near enough to fire cannons. From about a kilometre away you can hit a ship.

'SHOW YOUR TRUE COLOURS!'
This means flying your real flag. Raise the Jolly Roger – that'll scare them!

FIRE!
Fire just one cannon. Shout to the ship to surrender. Wait for them to reply or to raise a white flag, which means 'We surrender!'

IF THEY RESIST...

BOOM!
Fire broadsides (cannon fire across the length of the ship) to damage the hull and deck.

CRASH!
Fire barshot and chainshot (they're cannon balls linked in pairs with metal bars or chain) to rip through rigging, or knock down some sails or a mast. If they don't give in now, well…

BANG!
Draw closer. At 100m you can hit the crew with muskets. Use muskets to hit particular people, and use grapeshot (packs of small pellets, bits of metal and nails) to cause chaos on deck. If they don't give in now…

ATTACK!
The crew can hardly see anything through the smoke and chaos, and are coughing and spluttering. Your men can get on to an enemy ship from small boats.

GRENADES AND STINKPOTS!
Hand-thrown bombs like these can give off a terrible smell and smoke, as well as create dreadful damage.

GET THE GRAPPLING IRONS!
These are great big hooks on the end of poles. You hook them on to a ship and pull the two vessels together.

PREPARE TO BOARD!
Now the pirates leap aboard. The crew of the other ship won't stand much of a chance. Pirates appear over the sides from several directions.

BANG, BANG, BANG, BANG!
This isn't a kids' game. Pirates are shooting their pistols next to people – it's called point-blank range. Some are waving swords and axes around. Everyone grabs whatever they can hit anyone with. This is a fight to the death!

SURRENDER!
It could be minutes, it could be hours, but the pirates usually overpower their victims.

SURVIVORS?
The pirates might give their victims the chance to join their pirate crew, if they've put up a good fight. But, just as likely, the pirates throw any survivors overboard.

VICTORY!
You've captured your ship. Now what? Well, you could keep it as a prize and use it. You might burn it and sink it, if it's really badly damaged. You might sail it into a port and sell it.

BOOTIFUL BOOTY!
Now you've got to divide the booty – any treasure, valuable goods, anything you can sell. But be careful to share it equally … the crew might get cross, and decide to throw the captain overboard!

PAPER BOATS

DIFFICULTY RATING: ☠ ☠ ☠ ☠ ☠

This little boat is quick and easy to make. It will float for a little while, carry a bit of treasure and you can make a small fleet of boats – all in different sizes.

YE WILL NEED

- Square of paper 15cm or larger. A 21cm square cut from an A4 sheet is perfect

- Scissors

DID YOU KNOW?

PIRATE SHIPS NEED RESTS!

After a while a ship's hull gets covered with barnacles. They slow the ship and damage the timbers, so every now and then a ship has to be brought onto a safe beach for special cleaning, called careening.

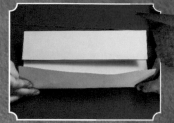

DIRECTIONS

1 Fold your square in half. Make a good crease. Open it out. From both edges, fold into the central fold.

2 Fold in half along the middle fold, with the flaps inside. Turn a corner up from the folded edge, so that it is about 1cm from the top edge. Repeat on the other end.

3 Make a fold along the top on both sides to make a line a little less than 1cm. On one side, this fold will hold down the corners you made in step 3. Open up the boat.

4 Gently shape the boat. Leave it as it is or pinch the base and make creases to make it sit better on the water.

Every pirate has to know how to 'read' a compass, because it tells you which direction you are travelling. This is especially important at sea, when you don't have many landmarks like trees and hills to aim for. With a compass, you know where you're going. Just turn it so that the N (north) lines up with where the needle points, and the other directions are set out clearly for you.

How to find north, south, east and west on dry land or at sea:

Wait until evening, and see where the sun is going down. That's west.

1 Stand holding your arms out wide, with your left hand pointing to the sun. That means north is in front of you. Your right hand is east, and south is behind you.

2 Usually the directions are abbreviated to letters – N, S, E and W, standing for 'north', 'south', 'east' and 'west'.

3 The points in between are easy to learn. Halfway between north and west is north west (or nor'west, in pirate-speak), NW. Halfway between north and east is north east (or nor'east), NE. Halfway between south and east is south east (or sou'east), SE. Halfway between south and west is south west (or sou'west), SW.

A MODEL PIRATE SHIP

DIFFICULTY RATING:

All the best pirates spend hours making models. Try making others in different shapes, sizes and with different sails. You could launch a whole fleet!

YE WILL NEED

- A piece of balsa wood 15mm thick, about 4cm wide x 12cm long (expanded polystyrene from some packaging might do, or normal wood, but you will need adult help with drilling holes and hammering in the drawing pins)

- Small pieces of thin card, cream or grey
- A4 sheet of paper
- 2 kebab sticks or very thin dowel rod
- Waterproof marker
- Drawing pins
- Blu-Tack
- Pencil
- Ruler
- Scissors
- Sellotape

SEE CUTTING DIAGRAM ON PAGE 94

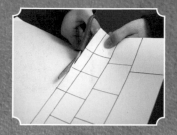

1 Draw the sails on a piece of paper. Then cut out all ten of them. Cut out all four card pieces A and B. With a waterproof marker, draw some parallel lines sideways about every 1cm.

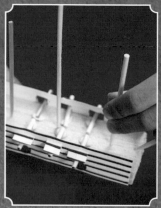

6 Mark where you want the masts to go, and push them in place. The longest one is the mainmast and goes in the middle. Push the smallest pieces at an angle in the front (to make the bowsprit) and the back.

2 On the other side of the two A pieces, draw three squares for the cannon holes. Fold the paper and cut in on the fold. Cut on the bottom and sides, but not the top.

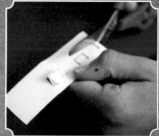

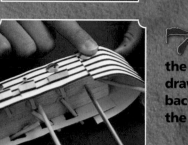

7 Fix the folded piece B at the front with two drawing pins. At the back, do the same with the curved piece B.

3 Cut the kebab sticks to make all the pieces in the diagram. It's easy to do with the scissors. Twiddle the stick in the scissors, then snap it in two.

8 Get the sails ready. Fold each in half, and cut a small nick on the fold about half a centimetre from the edges.

4 Fold one of the B pieces in half, and curve the other one. Fold up the cannon hole flaps on pieces A.

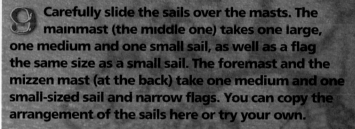

9 Carefully slide the sails over the masts. The mainmast (the middle one) takes one large, one medium and one small sail, as well as a flag the same size as a small sail. The foremast and the mizzen mast (at the back) take one medium and one small-sized sail and narrow flags. You can copy the arrangement of the sails here or try your own.

5 Fix one of the A pieces on to the balsa wood with two drawing pins. Fix the other piece A on the other side. Put the cannons in position with Blu-Tack. If you have a fine black marker, put a little dot on the end of the sticks first, to make the cannons look even more realistic.

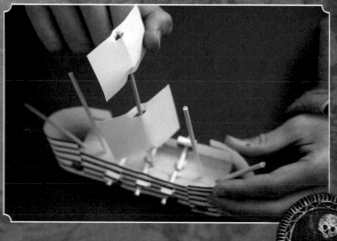

VITAL KNOTS FOR PIRATES

Any pirate sailing the high seas has to know how to tie knots! They are so useful – they tie things down, tie things up and hold things firm.

IMPORTANT!

Practising knots is good. Tying things up is fine, but tying people up isn't. It can be dangerous. So don't play around with knots unless you have adult supervision. Even tying string around your finger for fun can be dangerous. And never – ever – put string or rope around your neck.

TYPES OF KNOT

STOPPERS
Stoppers are in the middle or end of a rope and, for example, stop the rope slipping through a pulley.

BENDS
Bends join two ropes together.

HITCHES
Hitches attach a rope to something.

OVERHAND KNOT

Lots of landlubbers know this one. It's a good stopper, is very easy to do, but difficult to untie if it has been pulled hard.

FIGURE-OF-EIGHT

Pirates prefer this one. It's a better stopper, and easier to untie. It's great for helping pirates to climb rigging and pull up booty. You can use it for the tug-of-war on page 66, too.

REEF KNOT

Lots of landlubbers can do a reef knot. Pirates don't rate it much, though, because it jams solid when pulled very hard. It's also not very good for joining ropes of different thicknesses.

SHEET BEND

This one's better. It's easier to undo and is better at holding ropes of different thicknesses together. A sheet is the name for the rope that's tied to a sail. A sheet bend will make it hold safely to other ropes.

CLOVE HITCH

This is handy when you want to tie and untie something quickly. You could be in a rowing boat, making a secret visit on land. Tie up to a rail quickly and then be ready to get away fast, too!

READY FOR A QUICK GETAWAY!

BOWLINE

A bowline (pronounced 'bo-lin') holds something on to a post. Pirates and many landlubbers know this knot. It's a good 'un. Put the loop over a post to keep your boat, cow, horse or dog where you want it.

HOLD DOWN YOUR SAILS

MAKING A TELESCOPE

DIFFICULTY RATING:

Ship ahoy! The telescope was also called a spyglass or a 'Bring 'em near'. When you want to put the telescope away, just close it up. It pushes together 'telescopically' (the tubes fit into each other), so it can go in your pocket.

YE WILL NEED

- 28 sheets of A4 paper (scrap paper is OK), medium or heavy weight
- Piece of broomstick handle or 25mm dowel rod about 40cm long
- Masking tape
- Marker pen
- Black and gold paint
- PVA glue

'FULL AHEAD OR BRING 'ER ABOUT, CAP'N?'

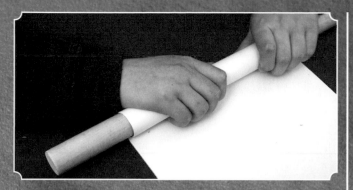

1 Take six sheets of paper and hold them together. Roll this set of sheets around your piece of wood, with the pages rolled on the width of the A4 sheet. Tape the paper in place.

2 With the pen mark a small line about 5cm from the left-hand end.

3 Take another six sheets of paper. Roll this second set over the first one, and tape it down to make another tube. Again, make a mark about 5cm from the left-hand end.

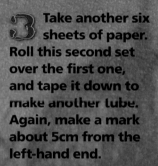

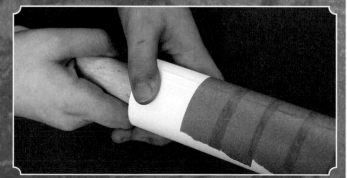

4 Take another six sheets of paper. Roll this third set over the second one, and tape it down on to itself.

5 You've now got three tubes of paper, which should fit snugly into one another. Pull them out carefully, and stop when you see the marks. Draw the lines all around the two smaller tubes.

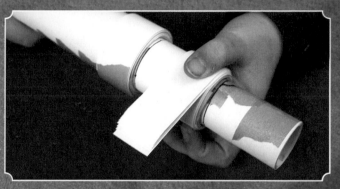

6 Cut ten sheets of paper to make sets of ten strips 21cm by 1.5 or 2cm wide. Hold one set of ten strips together and wind it around the telescope. Then stick it down. You need one set at one end of the two narrower sections of the telescope, and ones at both ends of the largest section.

7 Put a bit of glue around the strips to hold them down well.

8 Paint your telescope black. Then decorate it with gold paint or coloured paper.

PIRATES' PARTY GAMES

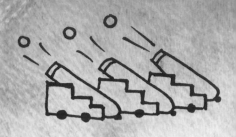

Gather together, me hearties! What d'ye want to play first?
Leave your daggers, swords and pistols by the front door,
and be ready for a wild time!

WALK THE PLANK

There is a wet version and a dry version of this game. For both, you will need adult help, and:

- long, narrow plank of wood
- something for it to rest on securely (for example, bricks, books, blocks of wood)

For either version you can blindfold the 'prisoners' with a long piece of cloth. However, make sure they are happy with this first.

THE WET VERSION

Fill a paddling pool with water. Put the plank across the pool, resting it securely at either end. Each person has to walk across and try not to fall in. If that seems too easy, make the prisoners walk across backwards next time! If that was too easy, as well, make them hop!

THE DRY VERSION

Put the plank between two supports (books, wood, etc.). Put down cushions on either side of the plank. Each person has to walk across and try not to fall off. Make the prisoners walk across backwards if they think this is too easy! Then make them hop!

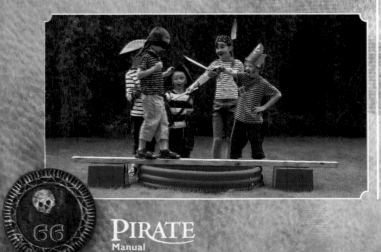

TUG OF WAR

Here's a wet version and a dry one.

- two teams of at least two pirates each
- referee
- rope, at least 4m long

Tie figure of eight (see page 63) knots all along the rope, roughly 30cm apart. Tape or tie a colourful piece of cloth or paper in the middle.

The two teams pull the rope with the marker cloth in the middle. You can stretch over a paddling pool or cushions.

Each team lifts their end of the rope. The referee says, 'Ready me hearties', and the teams pull the rope tight. At the command 'Heave', they pull as hard as they can. The winning team is the one that pulls the marker cloth over to their side – and the other team across into the pool or onto the cushions.

GAMES & PARTIES

CAPTAIN'S ORDERS

This is quite like the game 'Simon Says'. Someone is the Bosun, and everyone else is the crew. The Bosun tells the crew what the Captain's orders are. If they say 'Captain's orders... scrub the deck', you have to do it. But if the Bosun doesn't say 'Captain's orders' before giving the command, you stay quite still!

Here are some commands. You have to explain them to the crew first. You can also make up more orders of your own.

SCRUB THE DECKS .... Go on all fours and pretend to scrub the ground

UP THE CROW'S NEST .....Pretend to climb rigging

SALUTE THE FLAG................. Stand and salute

WEIGH ANCHOR ....Pretend to pull hard across on a rope in front of you

SHOW COLOURS .... Pretend to pull down on a rope to get flags up

PIPE 'EM UP .... Pretend to blow a whistle, make a whistling noise – this is what happens when sailors welcome a guest on board

BRING 'EM NEAR ....Pretend to look through a telescope

OVER TO PORT .... Everyone rush to their left

OVER TO STARBOARD .. Everyone rush to their right

TURN 'ER ABOUT...........Everyone turns round)

You can also play the game so someone ends up as the winner. You are out of the game if you make two mistakes – either doing the wrong action (and being spotted doing it) or doing an action when the Bosun has not said the magic words 'Captain's orders' first. If you are caught out twice, the Bosun calls out your name, like this, 'Lethal Lily, overboard with you', and you go to the side and watch.

CONTENTS

CARD GAMES FOR PIRATES

Pirates played loads of card games. On board, gambling was often forbidden. On dry land pirates could lose a fortune in one game! Keep your own treasure well away...

YE WILL NEED

PIRATE PETE

For 2–6 players:
- 2 standard packs of cards

UN, DEUX, TROIS

For 2 players:
- Standard pack of cards

PIRATE PETE

To start, choose as many pirate names as you have players (for example, six names for six players). Write these names on slips of paper, fold them up, and then shake them in your hands. Each player picks a slip of paper. That's their name until the end of the game.

You each have to learn everyone else's pirate name. (If it helps, leave the bits of paper on the table by each player.)

1 Deal the cards clockwise, face down. (If some players have more cards than others, don't worry.) No player can look at their cards – they keep them face down, in a pile.

2 The player to the left of the dealer starts play. He turns his top card over to start a pile of cards face up. All the others do the same, in turn, around the circle.

3 If a player spots that someone else's card is of the same rank as his (has the same number or picture), he has to be quick! Shout out the other player's pirate name twice (for example, 'Pirate Pete, Pirate Pete') before Pirate Pete gets to shout your name. The first player to shout correctly wins the other player's pile of face-up cards. He adds it to the bottom of his own pile of cards, held face down.

BEWARE!
Don't call out the wrong name! If you do, you have to give all your face-up cards to the player with that name.

4 The winner is the player who manages to collect all (or most, if you want to cut the game short) of the cards.

UN, DEUX, TROIS

This is rather like Snap. Remember: pirates are most interested in **diamonds**, and also need **spades** to dig for treasure. Young pirates play this game in French or in English.

Hold the top card ready. Both players say 'Un, deux, trois' (*un, derr, twa*) or, in English, 'One two three' and show your cards, placing them in front of you. You keep adding to the pile, showing cards one at a time together, until there is a match (or Snap). But you don't say 'Snap' – you have to look at the cards, and be ready to shout…

If **either** of you put down a **diamond**, shout, 'Mine!' or 'A moi' (*ah mwah*). The first one to say it wins that pile. He holds on to his own if the diamond is on his pile, or takes his opponent's if the diamond is there.

If **both** of you put down a **diamond**, the first one to shout 'All mine' or 'Tout à moi' (*toot ah mwah*) grabs **both** piles.

You can play it just like that, or add two more calls:

If **either** of you put down a **spade**, the first one to shout 'Dig' or 'A terre' (*a tair*, meaning 'to the ground') gets to dig and take the **top three cards** off the other player.

If **both** of you put down a **spade**, the first one to shout 'Treasure' or 'Trésor' (*tray-soor*) takes **all** the other player's pile.

The winner is the person who ends up with all the cards (or has the larger pile).

PIRATE MARBLE GAMES

DIFFICULTY RATING:

Pirates love to play marbles. But it's really hard playing on a ship that goes up and down with the waves. Marble games are much better to play when you are ashore, at home or in a tavern.

YE WILL NEED

COMPASS POINTS

For two players:
- 10 large marbles

BROADSIDES

For two players:
- 6 large marbles
- 20 small marbles

COMPASS POINTS

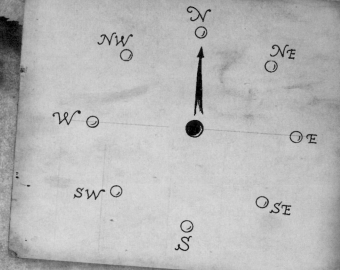

This is a game you can play on your own. You can also take turns with someone else. See who can go round the compass in fewer moves.

Set up nine marbles (as shown). Put them in a circle, about 40cm wide to start with. After some practice you will want to make the circle larger and the marbles harder to hit.

The shooting marble starts in the middle. What you have to do is hit all the marbles with this one, in the right order, in as few shots as possible.

When you hit the correct marble, the shooting marble goes to the centre again. Then you take the other marble away. If you miss, or hit the wrong marble, the shooting marble stays where it landed and you shoot again from there. You have to hit the marbles in this order, and call this out if you like:

North, **South**, **East** and **West**,
Pirates always shoot the best,
Nor'west, **Nor'east**, **Sou'west**, **Sou'east**,
Winners be that miss things least!

This game takes some practice. Can you keep beating your best score? Some pirates can do it in just eight goes – but can you?

BROADSIDES

'Broadside' means 'side on'. Think of this game as being like two ships, coming up to one another broadside. Imagine you're firing cannonballs at your opponent.

Set out the marbles as shown. These stand for your two ships. For each 'ship', the three large marbles are your masts and the ten small marbles are your cannons. In the golden days, five cannons per side wasn't bad for a small, quick pirate ship. A few large ships had many more. If you have enough marbles, set up longer lines. If you don't have many marbles, just lay out a single line of cannons.

Take turns shooting, one shot at a time. When you fire, you take any marbles you hit. If you hit, put your marble back in its original place for the next go. If you miss, you lose the marble to your opponent. If you hit a 'cannon' and there is another right behind it, you take both marbles.

Your first aim is usually to knock out your opponent's cannons. That way, your own ship is

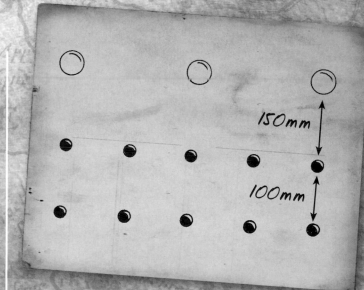

safer. Then you want to knock down the masts by hitting them.

The winner is either the first one to hit all the masts or to win the most marbles. As you get better, you can set your 'ships' further apart for further broadside battles…

PIRATE DICE GAMES

DIFFICULTY RATING:

Pirates gambled a lot on the throw of the dice. They often found safe places to stay where the locals spoke Spanish. Here's a game where you learn to be a mean pirate and learn some Spanish too!

YE WILL NEED

For 2–6 players:
- 2 dice
- 1 'ship' or playing piece per player (you can make your own – see 'Target practice' on page 36 to make these sails).
- 4–6 counters per player

PAY UP PLEASE

You need to learn some more Spanish for this game (it might be useful for holidays as well as voyages!). What you have to do is get as much loot as possible and boot out the other players. You have to be cold-blooded – but remain polite!

Each player starts with **two counters**. The other counters go in a pile in the middle. These are the pirates' treasure hoard of pieces of eight. Each player also has **one ship** or playing piece which starts in front of them. It doesn't move at first, but stays at anchor.

Each player throws the dice. The person with the highest score starts the game, then throws again.

STAGE 1
SHARING THE LOOT

At first you want to get one of two results:

● **Combined score of 8** – for example, a 3 and a 5. If a player gets 8, they call 'Ocho' (pronounced *o-choh* – which means 'eight') and picks up one counter (a piece of eight) from the pile in the middle.

● **Double 2** – at this the player calls 'Doble' (*doh-blay*, 'double') and can pick up two counters.

After a few rounds, there'll be no treasure left. Once that has happened, the game gets nasty!

STAGE 2
SETTING SAIL AND GRABBING THE LOOT

Now your ship (playing piece) sets sail. On your go, move it to stop by the player to your left. From now on, on each player's go, he moves his ship one step clockwise to sit in front of another player. The ships move only one step at each person's go. They don't move, like in Monopoly for example, according to the number on the dice but just to the next person clockwise. Remember to move your ship before your throw the dice!

● **Combined score of 8** – at this, the player points his fingers like a pistol at any other player. He calls 'Pagar por favor' (*pa-gaahr poor favoor*, 'pay up, please') and gets one piece of eight. Play moves to the next person. The player that is raiding must always be polite. He must say 'Gracias' (*grah-thee-ahss*, 'thank you') when he receives his treasure. If he forgets to say it, he may have to return the counter to the other player, plus an extra one! This only happens if the other player manages to say 'Volver' (*vol-vayr*, 'give back') before the next roll of the dice.

● **Double 2** – almost the same thing happens. You can win two counters, but only from the player next to your ship as it moves around. You call 'Pagar por favor' (*pa-gaahr poor favoor*, 'pay up, please') and get one piece of eight. And if you forget to say 'Gracias' and the other person remembers to say 'Volver', then you have give back two counters, plus another two. So watch out!

● **Double 6** – aargh! The player calls 'Perder!' (*pair-dair*, 'lose') and takes all the treasure from the person next to your ship counter. He doesn't even have to say sorry or thank you. That player is now out.

When you lose all their counters, you are out of the game. The winner is the pirate who takes all the treasure. If you're getting bored, however, you can just stop and count to see who has won the largest pile of 'treasure'. That person becomes the winner.

PIRATE
Manual

TREASURE MAPS

Planning to bury some treasure? Pirates often relied on home made maps to find their way back to hidden treasure. Some were very accurate but usually they were very rough though they all were meant to give you a good picture of where things were. Here are some ideas for making your own treasure map...

YE WILL NEED

- Sheet of paper
- Pens
- Pencils
- Marker pens

TORN EDGES

Tear the edge roughly to get a good wiggly shape. Or hold a ruler about 1cm from the edge of the paper, and carefully tear the paper up against it. This produces a rough but straight edge.

STAINS AND MARKS

Stains and marks look great, but be careful they don't ruin your hard work! Before doing any writing, you can:

- Dip the paper in vinegar or tea, and then let it dry
- Splatter it with wine, beer or tea

Before or after you've drawn it, you can:

- Add drops of red food colouring or ink to make it look like blood – make people think there was a fight over it!

- Drip wax on it – then it will look like pirates have been studying it in a dark tavern.
- Singe it at the edges with a candle, but be careful! This can be dangerous – get adult help.

FINISHING OFF

For the final touches, how about one of these ideas?

- Fold your map up and open it up again several times – to make it look well used.
- Go out and play, come back in and don't wash your hands. Then handle the map and make a few grubby hand marks and fingerprints
- Bake it in a low oven to turn it brown. (Important: Try this out on another sheet of paper first, to get the timing right. Keep watching it every five minutes, and remove before it gets too brown.)
- Jump on it and rub it in the ground – to make it look like it was buried
- Roll it up and tie with a ribbon

DRAWING

Little pictures will look great on your map. Try these:

crossed swords

fir trees

mountains

hills

sea serpent

trees

sealife

Skull & Crossbones

Castle

Stockade

Ships

A USEFUL TIP

Pictures on a treasure map will look better if you imagine the light is coming from the top left. Think where the shadows could be. Use some simple shading, as well – for example, short lines in one direction about 1mm apart, or cross-hatching (lines that cut across at right angles).

TREASURE HUNT

Treasure hunts can be a serious matter for a pirate. Luckily, if it's for a party you don't need to keep your pistols loaded or your shovels sharp!

YE WILL NEED

- Paper, pencils and pens
- Containers
- Treasure

PIRATICAL CLUES

For a pirate treasure hunt, you will need to invent some really piratical clues. You can write them like a pirate in old-style writing on a bit of torn paper.

Write commands such as 'March 30 steps sou'west' (don't forget to provide them with a compass!). Or you can pretend you are on a ship and write something like 'Sail full ahead twenty steps, over to port (left) ten steps' or 'Starboard (right) 20 steps, and face the stern (look behind you)'. Use pictures to help – for example, draw a tree if that's where the clue is hidden, or an igloo if it is in the freezer!

You could also make a pirate map of part of your house or garden, giving places and clever clues. But, remember: *don't* show where the treasure is!

PLANNING THE TREASURE HUNT

It's more fun if two or three people set up the treasure hunt – you, another pirate and an adult, perhaps.

WORK BACKWARDS

Hide the treasure first and plan your hunt backwards. This might sound silly, but it's often easier to describe a place where you have hidden something if you work back from it. It's also good to have the best clues at the end. Try to make it really good and unusual. Think up some excellent hiding places and clues, as well.

PLANNING YOUR ROUTE

● Decide how many stages you want. This will depend on who is playing and where you are. Around ten clues is usually about right.
● The route is up to you. It is fine to go backwards and forwards, but be careful that people don't find clues meant for later in the hunt. If you give every clue a number, you can sort things out more easily if someone finds a clue too early!
● Note down where you put each clue. You can put your own secret marker that will help you find the clue – for example, something no one else would notice, like an old match.
● Keep a copy of the full list of clues, and the places where you left things. You may need to check things from time to time. Don't rely on remembering where you put something.

HIDING THE CLUES

Where can you hide clues? Lots of places!

OUTDOORS

● trees, branches and bushes (stick a little coloured ribbon on the clues if you want to make them easier to spot)
● under stones (mark stones with a dot with some chalk)
● under garden furniture or park benches
● in a crack in a wall
● sunk in a pond (use a jam jar weighted with stones, with some string floating up)
● under an outside mat
● under a rock in a garden
● hung on a clothes line

INDOORS

● under a table
● under a bed
● in the fridge, freezer, oven or washing machine
● inside an ornament, hidden in the frame, behind or on a picture
● in clothing – a jacket pocket, in a sock or shoe
● in a book or magazine
● behind a radiator
● over a door handle
● in a saucepan
● in a glass or mug

TREASURE

Make sure the treasure can be easily divided. That way everyone enjoys the hunt. Small things like sweets, marbles, polished stones and sharks' teeth are good rewards for everyone.

PROTECTING YOUR CLUES

Especially for outdoors, containers can be useful for your clues.

● food pots, like yoghurt pots or cheese tubs (add some stones to weigh them down)
● small fizzy drinks bottles (roll up your clue, put an elastic band around it and pop it in)
● sweets containers, like plastic Kinder eggs, Smarties tubes or boxes

For an outdoor hunt, use waterproof marker pens if you are using paper clues (because they may get wet).

CANNONBALLS AHOY!

This is a valuable game for improving your aim. You need two crews of two or more pirates. You will probably need to play this outdoors unless you have a lot of space somewhere indoors.

YE WILL NEED

- Cardboard boxes (banana boxes are ideal)
- 6 or more tennis balls or soft sponge balls
- 3 poles or thick dowell rods about 2m long

- Corrugated cardboard
- Duct tape
- Knife or scissors
- Marker pens

DID YOU KNOW?

PLEASE PAY PIRATES PROMPTLY!

Sometimes pirates got nasty if people were too slow to come up with ransom (the money to pay for a prisoner's release). They would chop bits off their captives, and sometimes would send the bits ashore. Urrggh! So, the next time someone says, 'I'm glad to see you home in one piece', just think how truly lucky you are!

1. Cut sails out of corrugated cardboard (make them as big as you like). Cut slits in the sails – about 8–10cm) so the broomstick handles can fit through. Decorate them. Then tape in place.

2. The attacking crew stands about 10m away, or as far as you think best.

3. The defending crew gets ready to fight off the tennis balls (cannonballs) with their hands. They should kneel behind the boxes (the boat), in front of the sails.

4. The attacking crew tries to hit the sails and knock them sideways. They also want to throw cannonballs into the boat. Don't aim the balls at people's faces. The defending crew tries to protect the sails and stop any balls falling in the boxes.

5. When the attacking crew has run out of balls, the crews swap over. You can keep score if you want – note down who knocked down the masts and got balls in the ship. However, most pirates prefer just chucking the cannonballs at the ship!

BEWARE!
If you get too good at it, someone may try to kidnap you, as pirate crews always want someone with a good aim!

PIRATE INVITATIONS

Want to invite your crew to a pirate party? Well, here's your big chance to do some fantastic writing and drawing!

- Your invitations can be a scary sealed letter. Fold up your invitation and ask an adult to help you seal it with some red wax (or roll it up and tie it with a red ribbon)

- You can write it with funny spellings, just like a pirate (see below).

- You can use pictures – for example ships, skulls and crossbones, and a map (see treasure map on page 74).

Here's the kind of thing you could write…

Cap'n Tim Terrible calls his crew together on Tuesd! 24th June for a Piratical Party with enormous Enjoyment and muddy Mirth! Ye must meet at his Howse at Six of the Clocke. Black Spot if ye don't come!!

Awful · Annie · · commands · thee · · to Attend · her · Partie · · ye date be · 5th Jan.y · · ye time be · 3 · Bells · · ye place be · 75 ye Gardens · · Sail home at 6 Bells ·

COOKERY RULES FOR PIRATES

Pirate cooks were good at keeping their muskets and daggers clean. They were always ready for a fight. But they weren't so careful about keeping things clean and safe in the galley (ship's kitchen). Yet it's very important. 'Clean and careful' isn't exactly a pirate saying, but you must remember it if you want to avoid wounds and stay healthy!

Follow these rules (even if other pirates didn't)…

- **Always** wash and dry your hands thoroughly before preparing food and after touching raw meat.

- **Always** be very careful with knives. **Never** play around with them.

- **Always** turn off an oven or hob ring as soon as you've finished with it.

- **Always** clean work surfaces thoroughly before use.

- **Always** wear oven gloves when touching anything going in or out of an oven.

- **Always** put hot pans and dishes on a heatproof surface or stand.

- **Always** turn pan handles to the side on a hob. **Never** leave them sticking out, because you might knock them.

- **Always** be extra careful with hot liquids and steam, as these can burn badly. **Never** reach across a hot pan, and always take special care when draining hot food and wait for things to stop bubbling.

- **Always** clear up after cooking. Make sure you leave everything shipshape (neat and clean), so the chief cook in your home doesn't throw you overboard!

FRESH FOOD ON BOARD? YOU'D BE LUCKY!

Usually the food was really, really old. Cooks would hide the horrible taste of rotten meat and fish with strong spices. Yuck!' What with that and not much water on board (nobody bothered to wash much), life on board really stank. What's more, most of the men had to go to the toilet off the side of the boat!

Pirates sometimes kept live turtles on board for eating. They were easy to spot from the crow's nest, quite easy to catch at sea and really easy to catch on shore. The poor things were often kept in the hold for several weeks before they became someone's dinner.

Question
WHAT'S ORANGE AND SOUNDS LIKE A PARROT?

Answer
A CARROT!

CHAPTER 6

GRUB'S UP

CONTENTS

TIDDLERS' SCRAMBLE

DIFFICULTY RATING:

On board a pirate ship, you might find chickens, kept for their eggs, and cows, kept for their milk. With plenty of time on your hands, you would probably learn to be good at fishing, catching big fish and little ones – tiddlers! So here's a tasty dish containing all three ingredients – eggs, milk and fish. It's a good teatime snack, very easy to make and full of protein – to make young pirates big and strong!

YE WILL NEED

- Slice of bread
- Butter or margarine
- 1 or 2 eggs
- Dessertspoon milk
- Tinned fish of your choice (such as a couple of anchovies, 1 sardine, 1 herring, etc.) or small pieces of smoked salmon

SERVES 1

1 Toast the bread. Then spread with butter or margarine.

2 Make sure the fish is chopped into small pieces.

3 Break the eggs into a bowl. Then mix them up with a fork and add the milk.

4 Put a knob of butter or margarine into the saucepan, and heat gently until sizzling. Pour in the egg mixture and stir.

5 Add the fish bits when the egg is still a bit runny.

6 When the mixture has reached the firmness you like, serve on the toast.

POTATO BOATS

DIFFICULTY RATING:

These potato boats sail on a red sea – they look cool and taste great. The real Red Sea once was popular with pirates, as there were many ships loaded with treasure sailing there between Arabia to India.

YE WILL NEED

- Chunk of cheddar cheese
- 1 regular tin of cream of tomato soup
- 1 or 2 medium-sized potatoes for baking

SERVES 1-2

4 About 10 minutes before they're ready, empty the soup can into a saucepan. Simmer the soup, but do not boil it.

5 Using an oven glove, take the potatoes out and check they are ready. Take a thin kitchen knife and poke it down into a potato. If it goes in easily, your potatoes are probably cooked. If you have to push harder, they may need a few more minutes.

1 Preheat your oven to 200°C/400°F/gas mark 6. Cut some thin slices of cheese, about 3–5mm thick and 100mm square. This takes practice. Cut these slices in half, to make large triangles.

6 When ready, take the potatoes out of the oven. Let them cool on dinner plates for a couple of minutes. Holding them with the oven glove, cut a slit on the top of each half-potato. Put the cheese sails into the slits. Pour the soup on your plate or bowl, to make a tasty red sea.

2 Wash the potatoes thoroughly. Cut them in half lengthways and then take a little slice off their round bases, so they stand firmly.

3 Put them on a baking tray and place them in the oven for 45 minutes.

PIRATES' PUDDEN

DIFFICULTY RATING:

This is a tasty way of rounding off a meal. On land it's usually called bread and butter pudding. But you may like to say it the pirates' way: 'Ere's bre'n'baarr pudd'n fer yer tea!

THE FARE HERE IS FIT FOR KINGS! AAARR!

YE WILL NEED

- 4 slices white bread
- butter or margarine to spread on the toast
- 4 tablespoons currants or sultanas
- 300ml milk
- 50ml regular (not thick) double cream
- 4 tablespoons white or brown sugar

- 1 medium or large egg
- Nutmeg, grated
- ½ teaspoon vanilla essence
- Round baking dish or tin about 25cm diameter, or rectangular baking dish or tin, capacity 1.2litre/ 2 pint or more

SERVES 4-6

ADULT HELP NEEDED

PIRATE
Manual

1 Preheat the oven to 180°C/350°F/gas mark 4. Grease the baking dish well – wipe butter or margarine all over the inside, using a bit of kitchen paper.

2 Butter the slices of bread. Cut each slice in to quarters. Make a bread layer on the bottom of the baking dish. Scatter half the currants over this layer.

3 Cover with another layer of bread slices, and scatter the rest of the sultanas.

4 Put the milk in the measuring jug. Add the double cream. Stir in the sugar and vanilla.

5 Beat the eggs in the small basin. Add this to the milk mixture. Stir well.

6 Pour all this over the bread. Grate a little nutmeg over it.

7 Bake in the oven for 30–40 minutes. If you like, decorate the pudden with more sultanas or currants before serving.

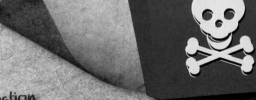

MAGGOTS ON TACK

Urrggh! 'Tack' or 'hardtack' was a name for horrible dry biscuits that the crew had to eat on board ship nearly every day. They were stored in biscuit barrels which were infested with creepy crawlies called weevils. Maggots and other horrid things ate into much of the food. Here's how to add maggots to your menu... Yum, yum!

YE WILL NEED

- Icing sugar
- Red or pink food colouring
- Icing syringe with a nozzle small enough to make thin lines (or use ready-made pink icing in a tube)
- Biscuits – rich tea or digestive
- Small drill bit

2 Sift ten table-spoonfuls of icing sugar into a bowl. Add one drop of pink or red food colouring into a small glass of water. Put three teaspoonfuls of this mixture into the icing sugar. Mix this thoroughly with a wooden spoon. If it seems too thick, add a little more coloured water. If it is too sloppy, add some more sifted icing sugar. Put the mixture into your icing syringe.

1 Wash the drill bit thoroughly – rub in washing-up liquid all over, rinse thoroughly and dry. Make maggot holes in the biscuits by gently twirling the drill bit (with your fingers) into the biscuits.

3 Squirt some small maggots on the biscuits next to the holes you have made – as many as you like. You can also make some greyish maggots by adding a little cocoa powder to the icing.

SQUAWKERS' PEG-LEGS

DIFFICULTY RATING:

'Squawker' is the name that pirates gave to prisoners who told them where their treasure was. But these peg-legs won't be squawking again!

YE WILL NEED

- 4 chicken legs
- 4 tablespoons tomato ketchup
- Small roasting tin
- Sunflower or mild olive oil
- Black pepper and salt
- Clean cloth or Kitchen roll

SERVES 3-4

3 Put two or three teaspoons of ketchup on each leg and spread it around with your fingers to make it look lovely and bloody. Your hands will probably get nice and messy – wash your hands before you scare anyone! Place the tin in the oven, and roast for 40 minutes.

NOTE

It's important that the chicken is fully cooked, so you don't get a nasty stomach ache. Cut into the meat of one of the peg-legs with a sharp knife, right to the bone. If the juices come out clear, they are cooked. If they dribble out pink or bloody, the legs need to be cooked a bit longer.

1 Preheat your oven to 200°C/400°F/gas mark 6 (this may take as long as 20 minutes). While it's heating up, wash the chicken legs under running water. Then wipe dry with a clean cloth or kitchen paper. Lay them on your roasting tin. Take a pinch of salt for each leg and scatter it all over. If you like black pepper, grind some over each leg.

2 Pour some ketchup into a bowl. Dribble a teaspoon of oil on top of each peg leg, and wipe it around with your fingers.

4 To finish, dot some fresh 'blood' (ketchup) on to the chicken legs. In the golden days, you might eat these chicken legs with dry bread or even drier biscuits. Today, you may prefer cucumber.

SUSAN'S SHARP CITRUS SIP

DIFFICULTY RATING:

We get most of the vitamins we need by eating lots of fruit and vegetables. Pirates and other sailors in earlier times were often ill because of their bad diet. One illness was scurvy. This gives you swollen, bleeding gums and causes your teeth to fall out.

That was not good news for a pirate crew. Everyone in charge of a ship – pirate, trader or Navy ship – wanted to solve the problem. About 250 years ago, a doctor discovered that scurvy was caused by a lack of vitamin C. Then suddenly lemons, oranges and limes were on the menu on board ship, because they were a source of vitamin C.

YE WILL NEED

- Tablespoon
- Juicer
- 2 large oranges
- 1 lime
- 3 tablespoons water
- 2 teaspoons Granulated sugar

1 Juice the oranges and limes. Then put the juice into a jug or bowl. Add the water and the sugar. Stir well.

2 Taste it. If it is too sharp, add one or two more teaspoonfuls of sugar and another tablespoonful or two of water. Stir well and serve.

PIRATE
Manual

LUCY'S LOVELY LEMONADE

DIFFICULTY RATING:

Pirates didn't exactly live like princes. But on their travels they could sometimes get their hands on things that people at home had never seen. For example, lemons and cane sugar came from traders in the Caribbean and Africa. Vanilla was expensive and pirates might capture some in a valuable cargo.

YE WILL NEED

- 2 lemons
- White sugar (caster or granulated)
- Water
- Vanilla essence
- Tablespoon
- Juicer

1 Juice the lemons. Measure out how much you have. Use the tablespoon, and pour the juice into your bowl one spoonful at a time. Remember how many spoonfuls you put in. Times that by five, and that is how many tablespoonfuls of water you now need to add. Fill the other bowl with water.

2 Spoon out the water you need. So, for example, if you have five tablespoonfuls of lemon juice, you need twenty five of water. Put in one extra tablespoonful for luck.

3 How many tablespoons of lemon juice were there? Add the same number of sugar. Stir well, so the sugar dissolves.

4 Pour five tablespoonfuls of water into a glass. Put just one drop *only* of vanilla essence into a teaspoon. Put that in the water. Take one teaspoonful of the vanilla-flavoured water and add it to your drink.

5 Have a taste to check your lemonade. Is it too sharp? If so, add two teaspoons of sugar, and two tablespoons of water. When it tastes right, pour it into a jug ready for serving.

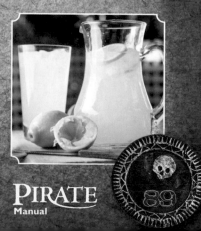

PIRATE PARTY CAKE

DIFFICULTY RATING:

ADULT HELP NEEDED

A pirate party wouldn't be complete without a special cake. You can decorate this with any edible jewels that you can find in your sweet shop and add some candles if it's for someone's birthday.

YE WILL NEED

CAKE MIX

- 175g/6oz softened margarine or butter (leave out of the fridge for an hour before cooking)
- 175g/6oz white sugar
- 3 eggs
- 1 tablespoon treacle

- 1 teaspoon vanilla essence
- Pinch of salt
- 80g/3oz cocoa, sifted
- 200g/7oz self-raising flour, sifted
- 6 tablespoons apricot jam
- Two sandwich cake tins, 18cm diameter

ICING MIX

- 1 heaped tablespoon cocoa, sifted
- 280g/8oz icing sugar, sifted
- Hot water
- Wooden spoon
- Bowl
- Sieve

If you have a food processor, you can mix all these ingredients in one go. Or you can beat them together using a wooden spoon or mixer in these stages:

- Mix the margarine and sugar well.
- Beat in the eggs.
- Mix in the treacle, vanilla essence, salt and cocoa.
- Stir in the sifted flour. Gently stir for a short time to mix thoroughly.

1 Preheat your oven to 190°C/375°F/gas mark 5. Line the tins with baking parchment (or, if they have a detachable base, grease them well). Divide the mixture evenly between the two tins.

2 Place mixture in the middle shelf of the oven for about 25 minutes. After 20 minutes, check if it is cooked. Stick a knife down in the middle. If the knife comes out clean, it's ready; if it comes out sticky, bake for another 5 minutes and test again. If still sticky, give it another few minutes.

3 Leave to cool, and then remove from the tin. Leave to cool further on a rack or plate.

4 When it is completely cool, spread apricot jam on one half and put the two halves together.

STICKY COCOA ICING

This is enough icing for covering either the round cake or the ship cake on the next page. It is sticky at first but dries quite hard.

1 While you boil some water, sift the icing sugar into a bowl. Sift the cocoa into the bowl.

2 Add three tablespoons of hot water, and stir together.

3 The mixture will be very firm at first. Stir until you get a good, even consistency for spreading. Add a little more water, a teaspoonful at a time, if it is too thick. Spread the icing on the cake when it is cold and firm, with a flat knife.

DECORATION

1 Cover the cake with sticky cocoa icing. Plan your pattern. Draw it on paper.

2 Roll out balls and thin sausages of royal icing on a board and roll them flat to get the shapes you want or press with your fingers. Roll it a bit, then lift it up and turn it. Roll it a bit more, until it is the thickness you want. You may need to add more icing sugar to the board to stop the icing from sticking.

3 Carefully lay down the icing pieces. Add more decorations, for example, Maltesers, chocolate coins and sugar diamonds.

GALLEON GÂTEAU

DIFFICULTY RATING:

This will certainly impress your shipmates! See what we've used to decorate the ship, but you can use coloured icing, special icing paints and different sweets or biscuits to create your own design.

The masts are made of breadsticks

Wafer paper for the sails, and edible ink markers

Red liquorice strings

Liquorice allsorts for the gun carriages

Cannons made from chocolate fingers (holes made with drill bit)

YE WILL NEED

- 175g/6oz softened margarine or butter (leave out of the fridge for an hour before cooking)
- 175g/6oz white sugar
- 3 eggs
- 1 tablespoon treacle
- 1 teaspoon vanilla essence

- Pinch of salt
- 80g/3oz cocoa, sifted
- 200g/7oz self-raising flour, sifted
- Knife
- Rolling pin
- Narrow drill bit
- Breadsticks
- Liquorice strings

- Liquorice allsorts
- Edible wafer paper (you can find this in specialist cake-decorating shops and some supermarkets) or normal paper
- Marzipan
- Cocoa
- Chocolate finger biscuits

PIRATE Manual

If you have a food processor, you can mix all these ingredients in one go. Or you can beat them together using a wooden spoon or mixer in these stages:

- Mix the margarine and sugar well.
- Beat in the eggs.
- Mix in the treacle, vanilla essence, salt and cocoa.
- Stir in the sifted flour. Beat for a short time to mix thoroughly.

1 Preheat your oven to 180°C/350°F/gas mark 4. Line the tin with baking parchment (or, if it has a detachable base, grease it well).

2 Spread all the mixture into the lined or greased cake tin.

3 Place in the middle shelf of the oven for about 50 minutes. After 40 minutes, check if it is cooked. Poke a knife down in the middle. If it comes out clean, it's ready; if still sticky, bake for another 5 minutes. Test again. If still sticky, give it another 5 minutes and test again.

4 Leave to cool. Remove from the tin and leave to cool further on a rack or plate.

DECORATION

Ask an adult to help you to cut the top of the cake flat if it is too rounded. Cut the cake into pieces (as shown).

Stick the sections together, using the sticky cocoa icing (shown on page 91) as glue. Spread icing over the top and sides.

Cut thin slices off the marzipan block. Roll them thinner to make pieces about the same height as the ship's side. Roll the black liquorice string into the marzipan to make even stripes. (We pulled liquorice wheels apart to get the black stripes for the sides.) Cut to make neat rectangles.

Stick these pieces to the sides, using the sticky icing and extra bits of marzipan. Now you are ready to put on all the fittings you want!

TREASURE CHEST

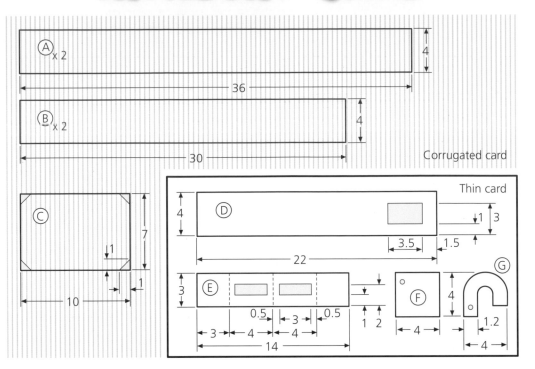

Corrugated card

Thin card

All measurements are in centimetres

A MODEL PIRATE SHIP

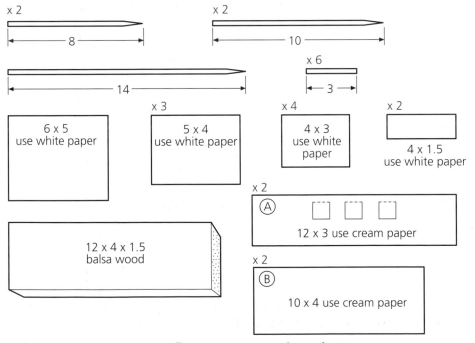

x 2   8

x 2   10

14

x 6   3

6 x 5
use white paper
x 3

5 x 4
use white paper

x 4
4 x 3
use white paper

x 2
4 x 1.5
use white paper

12 x 4 x 1.5
balsa wood

x 2
Ⓐ 12 x 3 use cream paper

x 2
Ⓑ 10 x 4 use cream paper

All measurements are in centimetres

A SIMPLE SCIMITAR

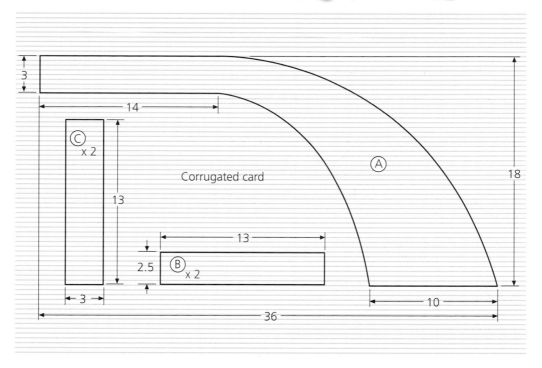

All measurements are in centimetres

A PIRATE'S CUTLASS

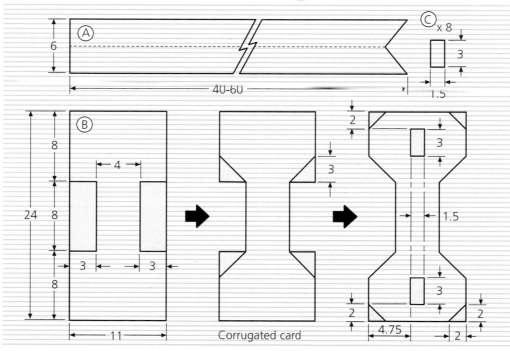

All measurements are in centimetres

A Midshipman's Dirk

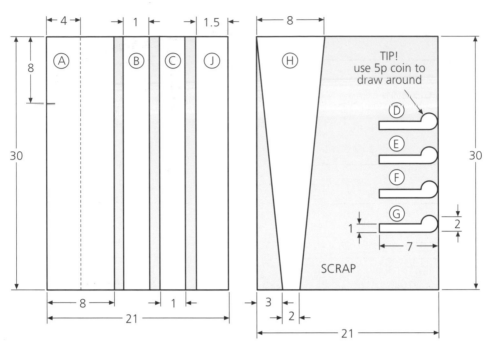

All measurements are in centimetres

Making an Axe

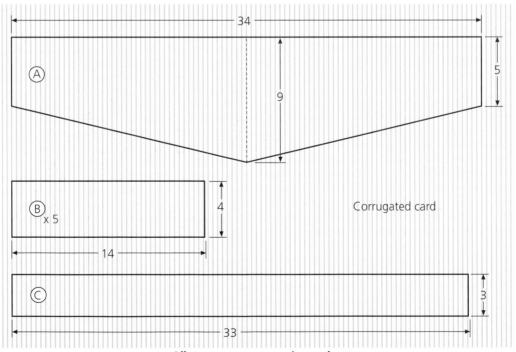

Corrugated card

All measurements are in centimetres

MAKING A CANNON

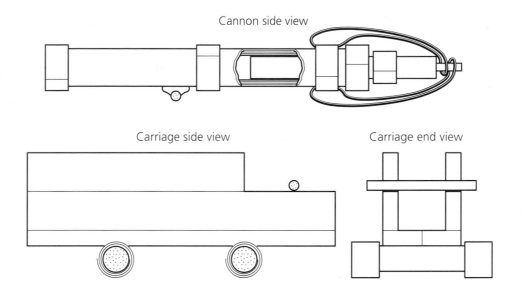

Cannon side view

Carriage side view   Carriage end view

All measurements are in centimetres

CANNON TARGET PRACTICE

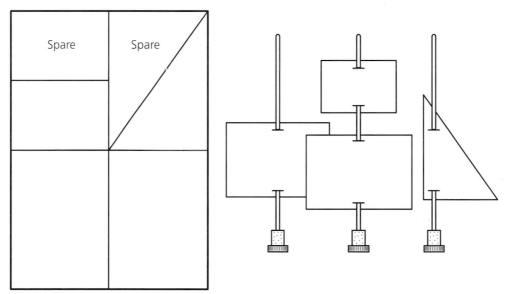

Spare   Spare

Use A4 sheet

All measurements are in centimetres

A CAPTAIN'S PARROT

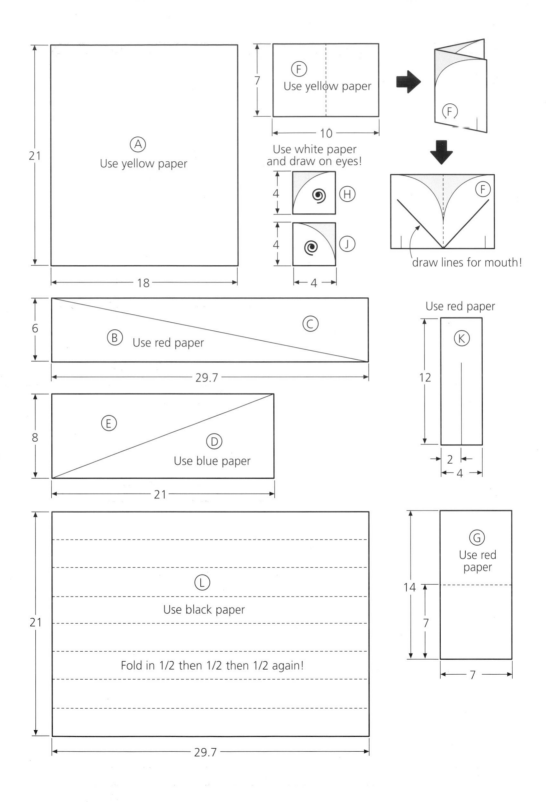

(A) Use yellow paper

21

18

(F) Use yellow paper

7

10

Use white paper
and draw on eyes!

4

(H)

4

4

(J)

4

(F)

draw lines for mouth!

(B) Use red paper (C)

6

29.7

Use red paper

(K)

12

2

4

(E)

(D) Use blue paper

8

21

(L)

Use black paper

Fold in 1/2 then 1/2 then 1/2 again!

21

29.7

(G)

Use red
paper

14

7

7

All measurements are in centimetres

PIRATE'S THREE CORNER HAT

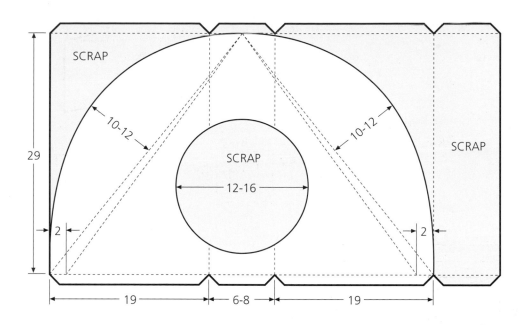

SCRAP

SCRAP

SCRAP

10-12

10-12

29

12-16

2

2

19

6-8

19

All measurements are in centimetres

TOMBSTONE HAT

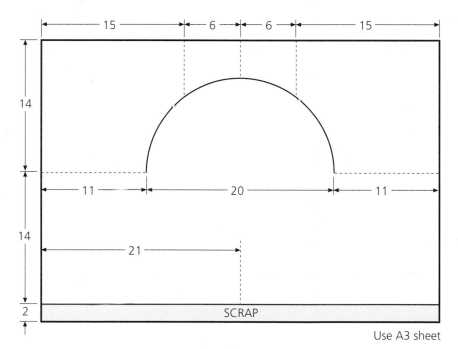

15

6

6

15

14

14

11

20

11

21

2

SCRAP

Use A3 sheet

All measurements are in centimetres

First published in October 2008

A catalogue record for this book is available from the British Library

ISBN 978 1 84425 550 4

Library of Congress catalog card no. 2008929391

Published by Haynes Publishing,
Sparkford, Yeovil, Somerset BA22 7JJ, UK

Tel: +44 (0) 1963 442030 Fax: +44 (0) 1963 440001
E-mail: sales@haynes.co.uk
Website: www.haynes.co.uk

Haynes North America, Inc.,
861 Lawrence Drive, Newbury Park,
California 91320, USA

Printed and bound in England
by J. H. Haynes & Co. Ltd, Sparkford

Author	Andrew Parkinson
Managing Editor	Louise McIntyre
Copy Editor	Nikky Twyman
Design	Lee Parsons, Richard Parsons
Layout	Richard Parsons, James Robertson
Photography	James Mann
Illustrations	Matthew Marke, Andrew Parkinson

We would particularly like to thank our young pirates for their excellent help: Debbie Allen, Joseph Allen, Ben Bailey, Daniel Bailey, Abigail Barnes, Annabel Barnes, Dion Bennett, Christina Dunn, Isaac Evans, Reuben Evans,Tom Evans, Philippa Gale, Tom Gale, James Hadderly, Tim Liebermann, Noah McIntyre, Ellie Rowles and Jacob Rowles

Photo credits

istockphoto.com p6, p9, p16, p20, p34, p50 (bottom), p51, p54, p55, p56 (both), p57 (top)
National Maritime Museum, Greenwich, London p7, p8 (both), p21, p50 (top), p57 (bottom)
© Osprey Publishing Ltd. Image from New Vanguard 70, The Pirate Ship 1660-1730, by Angus Konstam, illustrated by Tony Bryan, p52–53

Andrew Parkinson served on the Blue Peter when he was 12 (he has a badge of silver to prove it). Later, he looked for treasure while working as a landlubber for the British Museum. These days, his piracy is directed towards writing and when not sailing the high seas he lives in the well-known pirate county of Devon.

DORLING KINDERSLEY *CLASSICS*

Heidi

By JOHANNA SPYRI
Retold by Sally Grindley

Illustrated by **Pamela Venus**

A Dorling Kindersley Book

Heidi

Dorling Kindersley
LONDON, NEW YORK, SYDNEY, DELHI,
PARIS, MUNICH and JOHANNESBURG

Project Editor Natascha Biebow
Senior Art Editor Jane Thomas
Senior Editor Marie Greenwood
Managing Art Editor Jacquie Gulliver
Picture Research Victoria Peel and Jamie Robinson
DTP Designer Kim Browne
Production Joanne Rooke

First published in Great Britain in 1998 by
Dorling Kindersley Limited, 9 Henrietta Street, Covent Garden, London WC2E 8PS
Paperback edition published in 2000
2 4 6 8 10 9 7 5 3 1

ISBN 0-7513-7277-3

A CIP catalogue record for this book is available from the British Library.

Acknowledgements
The publisher would like to thank the following for their kind permission to reproduce their photographs:
a = above; c = centre; b = below/bottom; l = left; r = right; t = top.
Ace Photo Agency: Mauritius 29; Edmund Nagele 44 br; Ronald Toms 44-45; **AKG London:** 35, 46, 47 br; **Artothek:** Walter Klein 25; **Bridgeman Art Library, London/New York:** Elgin Court Designs Ltd, London: The Goatherd, c.1920 by Julius Paul Junghann (1876-1953) 10; **Britstock-IFA:** Bernd Ducke 31; **Jean-Loup Charmet:** 14; **Mary Evans Picture Library:** 45 tr, cl, 17 bl; Institution of Civil Engineers 46-47; **The Ronald Grant Archive:** Heidi, 1952 48 br; **Robert Harding Picture Library:** 45 tl; **Hulton Getty:** 45 bc, 47 cl; **Image Bank:** N. Romanelli 41, Hans Wolf 4; **The Moviestore Collection:** Heidi, 1937 © 20th Century Fox Film Corporation 48 bc; **Peter Newark's Military Pictures:** 48 clb; **Norfolk Rural Life Museum:** 45 br; **Rätisches Museum Chur:** 44 bl, 45 cr; ©**Retrograph Archive Ltd:** 19; **Roger-Viollet:** 47 tr; **Schweizerisches Landesmuseum Zürich:** 9, 12, 45 c; **Science & Society Picture Library:** 39; **Johanna Spyri Museum:** 48 tl; **Jürg Winkler (Museums-Stiftung Hirzel):** 48 cra.
Jacket: **Image Bank:** Hans Wolf back; **Johanna Spyri Museum:** inside back.

The publisher would particularly like to thank the following people:
Andy Crawford and Gary Ombler (photography); Sallie Alane Reason (additional illustration); Claire Ricketts (design assistance); Nick Turpin and David Pickering (editorial assistance); Lisa Lanzarini (jacket border); Marilyn Schaffner, Johanna Spyri Museum.

Colour reproduction by Bright Arts
Printed in China by L.Rex Printing Co., Ltd.

For our complete
catalogue visit
www.dk.com

Contents

Up the Mountain

ONE SUNNY June morning, Heidi trudged wearily up the mountain behind her Aunt Detie. It was very hot, but the little girl was wearing all her clothes at once as though it were winter. As they walked through a village, a voice called out, "Detie, isn't that the orphan your sister left? Where are you taking her?"

"I'm taking her to live with her grandfather," replied Detie. "I can't look after her any more because I'm starting a job in the city."

"Poor Heidi," said the villager. "No-one else will go near that miserable old hermit!"

While Detie gossiped with the villager, Heidi skipped away to play with Peter the goatherd. As he did every morning in the summer, Peter had come to the village to fetch the goats and take them to graze in the rich green meadows above. At first, he ignored Heidi. She scrambled behind him up the slopes, puffing and panting under the weight of all her clothes. Then she unwound her thick scarf, and took off her boots and both her dresses. She laid them in a neat pile and danced after Peter wearing only her petticoat. He couldn't help smiling then.

Heidi skipped away to play with Peter.

"How many goats have you got?" asked Heidi, and, "Where are you taking them?" She chattered away until they reached Peter's hut and Detie caught sight of her.

"What on earth have you been doing, Heidi?" she scolded. "And where are your clothes?"

"I don't need them," protested Heidi. "I want to run around free like the goats."

Detie tutted crossly and sent Peter back to fetch the clothes; then they carried on climbing. It took another hour to reach Grandfather's hut. Three huge fir trees stood behind it, and in front, on a wooden seat overlooking the valley, sat the old man.

Heidi ran straight to him and held out her hand.

"Hello, Grandfather," she said. He took her hand gruffly and stared at her intently.

"Good morning, Uncle," said Detie. "I've brought Heidi to stay with you. It's your turn to look after her now," she said, and explained why.

The old man stood up angrily and said, "My turn is it? Well then, you go back where you came from, and don't come here again in a hurry."

Detie quickly said goodbye to Heidi and ran off down the mountain.

"Hello, Grandfather," said Heidi.

The old man sat in silence, while Heidi explored her new home. She ran round the back and found an empty goat stall, then stood enjoying the sound of the wind whistling through the trees.

"Can I see inside now?" she asked, when she came back round to the front of the hut.

Her grandfather showed her into a biggish room with a table and one chair, a bed, and a stove. A cupboard in the wall held everything he owned. Heidi pushed her clothes right to the back.

"Where shall I sleep, Grandfather?" she asked.

"Where you like," he replied.

In a corner by his bed was a ladder. Heidi climbed up and discovered a hayloft filled with fresh hay. "I'll sleep up here," she said. "Come and see how lovely it is, Grandfather."

She shaped the hay into a mattress and pillow, while her grandfather brought her the covers from his own bed.

"Time to eat now I think," he said.

Heidi watched him toast a large piece of cheese over the fire in the stove. Then he sat Heidi on a three-legged stool and turned his chair into a table for her. On it, he placed a mug of milk and a plate with a slice of bread covered with the toasted cheese. Heidi couldn't believe how good everything tasted.

Mountain huts, like Grandfather's, had strong wooden frames and small windows to keep out the cold and wind.

That afternoon, she followed the old man everywhere, and watched as he carved a chair specially for her. When dusk fell, Heidi heard a shrill whistle and Peter appeared with his goats. With a shout of glee, she rushed to greet her friends of the morning. Two goats went straight to her grandfather, who held out salt for them to lick. Heidi patted them gently as Peter led the others away.

"Are these ours, Grandfather?" she asked. "What are their names?"

"The white one is Daisy and the brown one is called Dusky," replied her grandfather. "Now, young lady, it's time for bed."

"Good night, Grandfather. Good night, Dusky and Daisy," cried Heidi as she ran indoors.

Heidi was fast asleep.

That night, the wind howled so hard that the hut creaked and branches fell from the fir trees. The old man climbed up to make sure Heidi was all right. In the light of the moon he watched her sleeping, the expression on her face one of pure happiness.

Peter's shrill whistle woke Heidi the next morning. Eagerly, she jumped out of bed and ran outside, where Peter was waiting to collect Daisy and Dusky.

"Do you want to help Peter with the goats?" asked Grandfather.

"Oh, yes!" cried Heidi.

Grandfather gave Peter some bread and cheese for Heidi's lunch. "Mind you keep a close eye on her," he warned as they set off.

It was very beautiful on the mountain that morning. Heidi darted about picking flowers, and the goats, sensing her joy, ran here, there, and everywhere. Peter needed eyes all round his head to keep watch on them and Heidi.

In summer, goatherds led their herds up the mountain to feed on the rich grasses there.

At last they reached the foot of a rocky peak. Peter fell asleep in the sun while the goats grazed. Heidi gazed at the mountains above, which seemed to have faces like old friends. Suddenly, she heard a loud shriek overhead. "Peter! Peter! Wake up!" she cried. "Look at that bird! Why is it so noisy? Where is it going?"

"That's the hawk going home to its nest," answered Peter.

"Let's climb up and see where it lives," said Heidi.

"Not even the goats go that high," laughed Peter. "Come on, it's time for lunch."

Peter's lunch was tiny compared with Heidi's. To his amazement, Heidi gave him her share and seemed quite content with only two big mugs of Daisy's milk.

"What are the names of the goats?" she asked, while Peter enjoyed his feast.

Peter told Heidi about all the goats. She was sad when she heard that one of the little goats called Snowflake had lost her mother. Heidi promised to take special care of her.

By now the sun had begun to set, spreading a golden glow across the mountain tops. Heidi looked up in astonishment.

"Peter," she cried. "The mountains are on fire!"

"It's always like that," said Peter. "Tomorrow you can see it again. It's time to go home now."

During supper that evening, Heidi was full of questions. Grandfather said the hawk shrieked to tell people in the villages to stop making trouble for one another. He told her the names of the mountains and that the fire was the sun saying good night. That night, Heidi dreamed of mountains and flowers and of Snowflake.

Heidi darted about picking flowers.

All summer long Heidi went to the pasture with Peter. She grew strong and healthy and carefree as a bird. But when the autumn winds came, she had to stay at home. "We don't want you being blown off the mountain," said her grandfather.

So she spent the days watching him make cheese and build things with wood.

They flew down the snowy mountain.

Then the snows came. Heidi gazed out as the snowflakes fell faster and faster and buried the hut up to the window-sills. "I hope the hut will be buried completely so that we have to light a lamp during the day," she laughed.

Peter was at school during the week now, but one Sunday he came by to say his Grannie would like Heidi to visit her. Heidi begged to go the very next morning, but the snow was too deep. When the snow finally froze and the sun came out, Grandfather wrapped Heidi up warmly, sat her on his sledge, and they flew down the mountain, screeching to a halt outside Peter's tiny hut.

While Grandfather made his way back up the mountain, Heidi went inside. An old woman was bent over a spinning wheel.

"Hello, Grannie," said Heidi. "Here I am at last. Grandfather brought me on his sledge."

Grannie felt for Heidi's hand while Heidi looked about the room. "One of your shutters is hanging

Village women spun their own yarn from goat's or sheep's wool using a sturdy, wooden spinning wheel.

loose, Grannie," she said. "Grandfather will mend it for you."

"I can't see it, my dear, but I can hear it banging," said Grannie.

"Why can't you see it, Grannie?" asked Heidi.

"I can't see anything, child, light or dark, sun or snow. I shall never see them again."

Heidi began to sob. "Can't anyone make you see?" she cried.

"I can't see, but I can hear," said Grannie, softly. "Come and tell me what you and Grandfather do up on the mountain."

Heidi brightened up. "Just wait till I tell Grandfather about you. He'll be able to make you see, and he'll mend the hut, too. He can do anything." She chattered away about everything she did and how clever Grandfather was and all the things he had made, until Peter came in and walked her back up the mountain.

As soon as she was indoors, Heidi told her grandfather about the shutter and begged him to mend it and to make Grannie see again. "Well, we can at least stop the banging," he said.

All winter long, while Heidi kept Grannie company, Grandfather hammered and sawed. Little by little, he repaired the whole hut, but Heidi had to learn that he couldn't make Grannie better. ❁

"Here I am at last, Grannie,"
said Heidi.

Detie Comes Back

THE WINTER PASSED and another happy
summer. Towards the end of Heidi's second
winter, an old man dressed in black arrived at
the hut.

"Good morning, pastor," said Grandfather,
pulling up a chair for him.

"I'll come straight to the point," said the pastor.
"Heidi should have gone to school this winter. The
teacher sent you a warning but you didn't reply."

"She's not going to school," replied Grandfather. "She'll grow up

*"Heidi should go to
school," said the pastor.*

here with the goats and the birds, who
won't teach her any bad ideas."

"They won't teach her to read and
write, either," said the pastor.

The pastor did everything he could to
make Grandfather change his mind, but
Grandfather insisted Heidi should stay
with him up in the mountains.

The following day, however, they had
another visitor. It was Detie, dressed from
head to toe in fine new clothes. She

*In winter, village children
went to school to learn to
count, read, and write. In
summer, they had to help
their families earn a living.*

started to talk at once. "How healthy Heidi looks. You've certainly
looked after her well. Of course, I always intended to come back for
her. Anyway, now I've found a wonderful opportunity for her with a
rich family in Frankfurt. She's to be a companion to a little girl
who's confined to a wheelchair . . ."

"Have you quite finished?" interrupted Grandfather, rudely.
"Heidi's happy where she is."

Detie was furious. "Only someone who doesn't care about her

could keep her from such good fortune. You won't even send her to school or church. Well she's my sister's child and I'm still responsible for her."

"Then take her," thundered Grandfather. "But don't ever bring her back."

"You've made Grandfather very angry," said Heidi, as he stormed out of the hut.

"He'll get over it," said Detie. "Collect your clothes, you're coming with me."

"I'm not coming," said Heidi, "I want to stay here with Grandfather." But Detie was determined. She hauled Heidi off as fast as she could with promises that she could come back in a day or two with fresh rolls for Grannie. Heidi couldn't even say goodbye to Peter.

Detie didn't stop to talk to anyone in the village, and before she knew it, Heidi found herself aboard the train to Frankfurt.

Detie hauled Heidi off down the mountain.

When they arrived in Frankfurt, Detie took Heidi to a house belonging to a wealthy man called Mr Sesemann. His daughter, Clara, was an invalid. Her mother had been dead for a long time, and Mr Sesemann was often away on business, so Clara was left in the care of the housekeeper, Miss Rottenmeier.

When they arrived, Detie and Heidi were shown into the study, where Miss Rottenmeier came to inspect Clara's new companion. She was not impressed by Heidi's shabby dress and straw hat, and even less impressed by her name.

"Surely that's not your proper name," she said.

"She was christened Adelheid, after her mother," explained Detie.

"Then she will be called Adelheid," said Miss Rottenmeier. "And how old is she? I told you we wanted someone of Miss Clara's own age, which is twelve."

In the middle of it all, Heidi fell asleep.

Detie pretended not to be sure, but Heidi piped up, "I'll soon be eight. Grandfather told me so."

When Miss Rottenmeier learned that Heidi couldn't read, she shook her head in disbelief and said, "She really won't do at all." But Detie stressed that Heidi was just the sort of unusual child Miss Rottenmeier had said she was looking for, and quickly took her leave.

While Miss Rottenmeier was out of the room, Clara asked Heidi, "Do you want to be called Heidi or Adelheid?"

"Everyone calls me Heidi – that's my name," said Heidi.

"Then I'll call you Heidi," said Clara. "Are you glad you've come?"

"No," Heidi replied, truthfully, "but I

shall be going home tomorrow, with some nice fresh rolls for Grannie."

Clara laughed. "But you've come here to keep me company and to have lessons with me. They'll be much more fun now."

Miss Rottenmeier returned and snapped at the servants to serve the evening meal. Heidi was delighted to find a white bread roll by her plate. She asked one of the servants, Sebastian, if she could have it, and put it straight into her pocket. Then Sebastian held a dish of food out in front of her and she didn't know what to do, it was all so different from Grandfather's. Miss Rottenmeier launched into a long lecture on how she was to behave at the table, how she was to speak to the servants, and issued instructions about getting up, going to bed, shutting doors, keeping tidy, and so on and so on.

In the middle of it all, Heidi fell asleep. ✻

Heidi knows nothing about table manners. She's never even used a knife and fork. The white bread roll is a big treat.

Strange Goings-On

WHEN HEIDI WOKE the next morning in a big room in a high bed, she couldn't think where she was. Then she remembered – she had come to Frankfurt. She went to the bedroom window, but it was so high that she could only just peep out. All she saw were the walls of the buildings opposite. Heidi began to feel frightened.

At breakfast, Heidi asked Clara, "How can I look out of the window and see what is down below?"

Clara explained that the servants would open a window for her if she wanted, then asked Heidi to tell her about her life at home.

Heidi chattered longingly about the mountains and goats and all the other things she loved, until Clara's tutor, Mr Usher, arrived and began teaching Heidi the alphabet. It wasn't long before a tremendous clatter brought Miss Rottenmeier running.

Heidi asked a hurdy-gurdy player to show her the way.

"Heidi thought the carriages were fir trees rustling and knocked over the ink in her rush to see them," said Clara, smiling behind her hand.

"Does she think Frankfurt is in the middle of a wood?" exclaimed Miss Rottenmeier.

She stormed off to find Heidi and scolded her roundly.

That afternoon, Heidi was relieved to learn she could do as she liked while Clara rested. She asked Sebastian to open a window. "There's nothing but stony streets," she said sadly. "Where can I go to see the whole valley?" she asked.

"Somewhere high, like that church tower over there," Sebastian told her.

Heidi ran out of the house to find the church

Poor city boys often earned a living by playing a hand organ called a hurdy-gurdy. It made music when the handle was turned.

tower but soon got lost. She asked a hurdy-gurdy player to show her the way. "Clara will pay you if you come to the house," she promised.

When they got to the church tower, Heidi begged the keeper to let her climb up. But all she could see from the top were chimneys and roofs. Seeing how disappointed she was, the keeper showed her a basket full of kittens. "You can have them," he said. "I'll deliver them to your house."

"Oh, yes, please," said Heidi. "Can I take two of them now?"

The keeper nodded. Heidi put the kittens in her pocket and skipped back home. When she got inside, she found everyone in the dining-room waiting to eat. "Why did you leave the house without permission?" asked Miss Rottenmeier severely.

"Miaou," seemed to be Heidi's reply. "Miaou, miaou."

Miss Rottenmeier almost choked with anger. "How dare you make fun of me!" she screeched.

"It's not me, it's the kittens," Heidi protested, and held them up.

Miss Rottenmeier screamed and ran from the room. She was terrified of cats. But Clara adored the kittens. She begged Sebastian to hide them, so she and Heidi could play with them later.

"Leave it to me, Miss Clara," said Sebastian, chuckling.

All Heidi saw from the tower were chimneys and roofs.

The next morning, Sebastian went to the front door to find a ragged boy with a hurdy-gurdy on his back, holding a tortoise.

"I've come for the money Clara owes me," he said.

Miss Rottenmeier hates cats, but other families kept them to chase away mice and rats that ate their food stores.

"How can Miss Clara owe you money?" asked Sebastian, rudely.

"I showed her the way to the tower yesterday," said the boy. Sebastian began to grin.

"What's Heidi been up to this time?" he wondered. "All right," he said out loud. "I'll let you in if you'll play a tune for Miss Clara." He led the boy to the study, where Clara and Heidi had begun their lessons. The boy set down his tortoise, and began to play.

In a room close by, Miss Rottenmeier pricked up her ears. "Where's that dreadful noise coming from? It sounds as if ..." She ran to the study and stood by the door, horror-struck. "Stop that at once!" she cried. She ran across the room and tripped over the tortoise, then screamed for Sebastian who, doubled up with laughter, put some coins into the boy's hand and led him away.

Before Miss Rottenmeier could find out who was responsible for this latest outrage, Sebastian reappeared with a big basket for Clara.

"For me?" said Clara in surprise.

"Finish your lessons first," said Miss Rottenmeier.

Clara didn't have to wait long to find out what was inside the basket. It wasn't fastened properly, and suddenly there were kittens everywhere. They bit Mr Usher's trousers, climbed up Miss Rottenmeier's skirt, and scrambled onto Clara's chair.

"Oh, aren't they pretty little things!" exclaimed Clara.

"Sebastian!" screamed Miss Rottenmeier.

"Get rid of these dreadful creatures."

It wasn't until the evening,

when Miss Rottenmeier had recovered a little, that she got to the bottom of the morning's disturbances. She turned to Heidi, who was quite unaware that she had done anything wrong. "I can think of only one punishment for a dreadful child like you," she said. "Perhaps a spell in the dark cellar among the bats and rats will change your ways."

But Clara protested loudly. "Oh, please, Miss Rottenmeier. Wait till Papa comes home. I'll tell him everything and he'll decide what's to be done with Heidi."

Reluctantly, Miss Rottenmeier agreed.

"Get rid of these dreadful creatures," screamed Miss Rottenmeier.

For a few days there were no further mishaps. But Heidi was beginning to feel terribly homesick. Then she remembered that Detie had told her she could go home when she wanted. One afternoon, she wrapped up the rolls she had been saving, put on her old straw hat, and went to the front door. Just at that moment, Miss Rottenmeier saw her.

"Where do you think you're going, dressed like that?" she demanded.

"I want to go home to see Grandfather and Grannie," murmured Heidi.

"What? You'd simply run off? What's wrong with this house, pray? You're an ungrateful girl who doesn't know when she's well off."

Miss Rottenmeier scolded Heidi for trying to run away.

At this, Heidi burst out, "I want to go home because the goats and Grannie will be missing me and here I can't see the sun saying good night to the mountains, and if the hawk flew over Frankfurt he'd shriek louder because so many people are horrid and cross."

"The child's out of her mind!" exclaimed Miss Rottenmeier.

She called for Sebastian to take her to her room. He tried to cheer Heidi up by promising to take her to play with the kittens, but that evening Heidi didn't eat a thing, though she put a roll in her pocket as usual.

Coarse, brown bread is hard for Grannie to chew, so Heidi has been saving expensive soft, white bread rolls for her. She does not realize they will go hard and stale.

Worse was to come the following day. Miss Rottenmeier decided to give some of Clara's outgrown dresses to Heidi before Mr Sesemann came home. She went to look through Heidi's own clothes to see what was worth keeping. There, in the cupboard, she found the hoard of rolls. She immediately ordered one of the servants to throw them away, together with Heidi's old straw hat.

"No!" Heidi wailed when she heard what was happening. She threw herself down by Clara's chair and sobbed, "Now Grannie won't get any nice white bread."

Clara did her best to console Heidi. "I promise to get you just as many rolls as you have saved to take to Grannie when you go home. And they'll be soft fresh ones, not hard and stale ones like those you've been saving. Please don't cry any more, Heidi."

It was a long time before Heidi could stop crying, but at last she understood what Clara was saying and felt comforted. That night, when she went to bed, she found her old straw hat under the quilt. Sebastian had rescued it for her. ✽

*Mr Sesemann
arrived laden
with presents.*

Mr Sesemann Comes Home

THERE WAS great excitement in the house a few days later when Mr Sesemann returned from his travels laden with presents. He greeted Clara affectionately, then held out his hand to Heidi.

"So this is our little Swiss girl," he said. "Tell me, are you and Clara good friends? I hope you don't squabble."

"Clara is always good to me," said Heidi.

"And Heidi never quarrels with me," said Clara.

"Good," said Mr Sesemann. "Now as soon as I've had something to eat, I'll come back and show you what I've bought for you."

He went along to the dining-room, where Miss Rottenmeier greeted him with a face like thunder. "Things are not well here, Mr Sesemann. Heidi is quite unsuitable for Miss Clara. Her conduct is beyond belief, and you should see the sort of people and animals she has brought into the house. I can only think she's not quite right in the head."

"She seems normal enough to me," said Mr Sesemann, and then, as Mr Usher came into the room, he continued, "Perhaps you can help, Mr Usher. Tell me plainly what you think of Heidi."

"So this is our little Swiss girl," said Mr Sesemann.

Like this businessman being met by his children, Mr Sesemann is delighted to see Clara again. He is often away on business, but gives Clara lots of attention when he is home.

Mr Usher started rambling on about Heidi being behind in her education and a little unusual in her conduct, but he took so long to come to the point that Mr Sesemann excused himself and went to find Clara.

"What's been going on while I've been away?" he asked her.

Clara told him exactly what had happened, about the hurdy-gurdy player and the kittens, the rolls and everything else. When she had finished, her father laughed out loud.

"So you don't want me to send Heidi home?"

"Oh no, Papa," cried Clara. "Since Heidi's been here, delightful things have happened nearly every day."

Mr Sesemann went to find Miss Rottenmeier. "Heidi will stay," he said firmly. "The child seems perfectly normal and Clara loves having her here. If you find her too much to manage, my mother will be arriving soon and she can manage anyone."

Mr Sesemann was only home for a fortnight, but soon after he had left, a letter arrived to say that old Mrs Sesemann would arrive the following day.

"Since Heidi came, delightful things have happened," Clara told her papa.

Late the next day, Grandmamma Sesemann arrived. Heidi saw such a kind expression on the old lady's face that she loved her at once.

While Clara was resting the following afternoon, Grandmamma asked Miss Rottenmeier to fetch Heidi so that she could give her some books.

"Books!" exclaimed Miss Rottenmeier. "In all the time she has been here, she hasn't even learnt her alphabet, as Mr Usher will tell you."

"That's strange," said Grandmamma. "Well, she can at least look at the pictures."

Heidi soon appeared. She loved looking at the beautiful books. Then, all of a sudden, she burst into tears when they came to a picture of a green meadow with animals grazing, a shepherd, and a setting sun.

When she saw the picture of the green meadow, Heidi burst into tears.

"Come, my dear, don't cry," Grandmamma said gently. "Dry your eyes and we'll have a chat. Tell me, what have you learnt in your lessons?"

"Nothing," sighed Heidi. "Peter told me it was too difficult, and it is."

"But you musn't simply take his word for it. You must try hard yourself. As soon as you can read, I will give you this book."

Books were very expensive, so only rich people like the Sesemanns could own them. Heidi is upset because the picture reminds her of home.

Heidi's eyes shone when she heard this. "I wish I could read now!" she exclaimed, and for a few moments she was happy.

But Heidi had begun to realize that she couldn't just go home when she wanted to. She believed Mr Sesemann would think her ungrateful if she asked to go away, so she didn't tell anyone how she felt. When she was alone in her room, she often lay awake thinking of the mountains, and then she would dream about being home and wake up crying because she was still in Frankfurt.

When Grandmamma noticed her tears one morning, she asked her why she was so sad.

"I can't tell you," said Heidi. "I can't tell anyone."

"If we can't tell an ordinary person our troubles," said Grandmamma, "then we can tell God and ask Him to help us."

That night, Heidi knelt by her bed and begged God to help her go home.

❋

One morning, about a week later, Mr Usher came to Grandmamma with the news that Heidi could read at last. She went to the study to find Heidi reading to Clara. "I can do it!" exclaimed Heidi excitedly. "Now I can read stories about all kinds of people and things."

That evening, at supper, Heidi found the big picture book beside her place. "It's yours now," said Grandmamma, "even when you go home." ❋

Heidi was in the study, reading excitedly to Clara.

Home Again

WHEN GRANDMAMMA LEFT, strange things began to happen in the house. Every morning the front door was found wide open, even though it had been locked and bolted. Nothing was ever stolen and there was nothing to show who had opened it. Miss Rottenmeier asked Sebastian and John, the coachman, to spend a night downstairs to see if they could discover the cause of the mystery.

Evening came, and the two men sat up and waited, but there were no unusual sounds. At one o'clock, John went out into the hall to check. Almost at once, a gust of wind blew out his candle. "The front door is wide open," he stammered, "and there was a white figure on the stairs which vanished."

A cold shiver ran down Sebastian's spine.

As soon as Miss Rottenmeier heard their story, she wrote to Mr Sesemann asking him to come home.

Two days later, Mr Sesemann arrived home. He summoned his friend Doctor Classen to help him keep watch that evening. They chuckled at the idea of a ghost, but settled down to wait anyway. At about one o'clock in the morning, they heard the sound of a bolt being pushed back. They rushed out into the hall. The front door was open and a streak of moonlight shone on a white figure standing there.

"Who's there?" shouted Dr Classen.

The figure gave a little cry. It was Heidi, in her white nightgown.

"What are you doing here, child?" asked Mr Sesemann in astonishment.

"I don't know," answered Heidi faintly.

"I think this is a case for me," said Dr Classen. He took Heidi gently by the hand and led her upstairs to bed.

"Have you been dreaming?" he asked her.

"Oh, yes," said Heidi. "I dream every night that I'm back with Grandfather, and I get up to see the stars shining, but when I wake up I'm always still here in Frankfurt." Tears began to stream down her cheeks.

"Have a good cry," said Dr Classen. "Then go to sleep and in the morning everything will be all right."

He went to find Mr Sesemann. "Your ghost is Heidi sleepwalking," he said. "She's terribly homesick and has lost a lot of weight. You must send her back home – that's the only cure."

Mr Sesemann immediately began preparations for Heidi's journey home. Clara was very upset when she heard, but her father promised she could visit Heidi soon.

It was Heidi in her white nightgown.

Doctors often sent their patients to the mountains to rest – but Dr Classen sends Heidi back to the mountains because she's ill from missing her home there.

Heidi couldn't believe she was going home at last. Sebastian accompanied her on the long train journey, then arranged for her to travel to the village with the baker on his cart. Her arrival caused a stir among the villagers, who were amazed that she was going back to Grandfather of her own accord.

Heidi ran first to Peter's tiny hut, where Grannie was sitting in her usual corner. "It's Heidi, Grannie," she cried, and threw herself on Grannie's lap and hugged her. "I'll never go away again and I've brought you fresh rolls from Clara and I'll visit you every day," said Heidi.

"How wonderful!" exclaimed Grannie. "But you're the best present ever."

"I must go to Grandfather now," said Heidi excitedly. "I'll come again tomorrow."

Heidi continued her climb. Soon she could see her grandfather's hut. He was sitting on the bench outside, just like the first time she saw him. Heidi ran to him crying, "Grandfather!" and threw her arms round him. For the first time in years, his eyes were wet with tears.

"I've brought you fresh rolls," cried Heidi.

"So you've come back, Heidi," he said. "Did they send you away?"

"Oh no, Grandfather," said Heidi. She tried to explain what had happened, then from her basket she fetched a letter and a packet from Mr Sesemann. Grandfather read the letter and said, "The packet's for you, Heidi. There's money in it for you to buy a bed and anything else you may need."

"I don't need it," said Heidi, and then she cried excitedly, "but I can use it to buy fresh rolls for Grannie to have every day!"

Just then she heard a shrill whistle, and saw Peter with the goats. He stared at her in astonishment and said, "I'm glad you're back."

Heidi greeted the goats, then ran inside the hut, where she found that Grandfather had made up her old bed in the loft. That night, she slept soundly for the first time since she'd been away.

Grandfather woke her in the morning wearing his smartest clothes. "Put on your best dress," he said, "and we'll go to church together."

They set off down the mountain hand in hand, and when they entered the church, people turned to stare at them. At the end of the service, Grandfather spoke to the pastor. "I have changed my mind. I shall move down to the village for the winter so that Heidi can go to school."

The pastor smiled, and the villagers saw them part like old friends. They crowded round them. "We're so pleased to see you among us again," they said.

When they started back home, Grandfather said to Heidi, "I never thought I would be this happy again. It was a good day when God sent you to me."

After the service, Grandfather spoke to the pastor.

As dawn broke one September morning, Heidi was woken by a fresh breeze rustling the tops of the fir trees. She leapt out of bed and went to watch her grandfather milking Dusky and Daisy. Peter soon came up the path with the rest of the goats and asked, "Are you coming with me today?"

"I can't, Peter," said Heidi. "My nice people from Frankfurt might arrive."

She had been saying the same thing for days, and Peter was fed up with it. He went grumpily on his way, while Heidi spent the morning tidying the hut. When she came out, she looked down the mountain slope and cried, "Grandfather! They're coming!" She had recognized the doctor and rushed to greet him. "Doctor! Thank you a thousand times for sending me home to Grandfather." Then she looked down the path and asked, "Where are Clara and Grandmamma?"

"I'm afraid I've come alone," said Dr Classen. "Clara has been very ill and isn't fit to travel. They'll come in the spring when it's warmer."

Heidi was thrilled with all the wonderful gifts.

Heidi and Grandfather eat simple, wholesome food, such as brown bread and cheese. The sausage the doctor brought is a luxury.

Heidi was very upset at first, but brightened up at the thought of showing the doctor all the things she loved. "Come and meet Grandfather," she said.

The two men shook hands warmly and sat down with Heidi on the seat outside the hut. "I hope you'll spend as many of these beautiful autumn days as you can up here," said Grandfather. "I'll be your guide over any part of the mountains you wish to see."

He disappeared indoors and soon brought out a steaming jug of milk and golden cheese. The doctor ate his meal with great relish and said, "This is certainly the place for Clara to come to get well."

Just then a man arrived with an enormous parcel. "Ah," said the doctor. "Now you can have fun unpacking your gifts from Clara."

Heidi was thrilled when she found cakes and a shawl for Grannie, a huge sausage for Peter, tobacco for Grandfather, and all sorts of surprises for herself.

The weather was glorious all that month. The doctor came up to the hut every day from the village where he was staying. Sometimes he went off on long walks with Grandfather who told him all about the plants and wildlife. Other days Heidi took him up to the pasture, where she chattered away about the goats and the mountains, or recited verses she had learnt by heart.

All too soon it was time for the doctor to return to Frankfurt. Heidi walked a little way down the mountain with him, until he stopped and said, "I wish I could take you back with me to Frankfurt."

Heidi thought for a moment and replied, "It would be nicer if you came back to us." ❁

Winter in the Village

GRANDFATHER KEPT his promise to move to the village in the winter so that Heidi could go to school. As soon as the first snow fell, he took Heidi and the goats down to the village, where they rented a ramshackle old house that he had spent the autumn repairing. Heidi eagerly explored all over, until she came to a room with panelled walls and a huge white stove in the corner. Behind the stove was an alcove, and there was her bed, made up just as it had been at the hut. "Oh, Grandfather," she exclaimed happily, "my room! Isn't it lovely?"

Heidi missed the mountains, but she soon felt at home. Each morning, she leapt out of bed to visit Dusky and Daisy in their stall at the back. Then she went off to school and worked hard at her lessons.

Peter was hardly ever at school. One lunchtime, when he burst in to tell Grandfather that the snow was now hard enough for Heidi to visit Grannie, Heidi asked, "Why weren't you at school again today?"

"I couldn't stop the sledge and went straight through the village," said Peter dramatically, "and then it was too late."

"Do that again and

Heidi went to school and worked hard at her lessons.

you'll get what you deserve from me," said Grandfather sharply. "Now have something to eat, then Heidi can go and visit Grannie."

When Heidi climbed back up the mountain with Peter, she was upset to find Grannie ill in bed. She did her best to cheer her up by reading hymns, and that night she lay in her own bed thinking that if only she could read to her every day she might help to make her better. Then she had an idea that pleased her so much she could hardly wait till morning to carry it out.

Peter went to school the next day. On his way back, he dropped in at Grandfather's as usual. As soon as he was inside, Heidi caught hold of his arm and said excitedly, "I've thought of something. You must learn to read properly."

"Can't be done," said Peter.

"I'm going to teach you," said Heidi, "and then you can read to Grannie every day, especially when the snow is too deep for me to visit her."

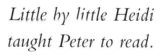

Little by little Heidi taught Peter to read.

Peter refused at first, but when Heidi pointed out the problems he would have if he didn't learn, he at last agreed. With the rhyming ABC book that Clara had given her, Heidi taught Peter the alphabet, then a few words, until one day, he astonished Grannie by reading her a whole hymn. Soon the whole village heard how Grandfather was responsible for getting Peter to school, and how Heidi had taught him to read. ❋

Peter is convinced he will never read, but Heidi helps him learn his letters with an alphabet book like this. Once he knows his ABC, he can sound out words, then sentences.

The Unexpected Happens

As SOON AS spring came and the mountainsides were green again, Heidi and Grandfather moved back to the hut. Heidi gleefully explored her old haunts until Peter arrived with a letter from Clara. Heidi read it out. "They'll be here in just over six weeks' time," she said excitedly.

The prospect of more visitors from Frankfurt made Peter angry. Grannie too seemed troubled when she heard the news. She feared that Heidi's friends would take her away again. But Heidi knew nothing of this, and could hardly wait for the end of June. At last, one morning she went out of the hut and suddenly shouted, "They've come! They've come!"

Grandfather saw two men carrying a chair on poles and on it a little girl carefully wrapped up. Behind them rode a stately woman on horseback, while two more men pushed a wheelchair and carried an enormous bundle of rugs. Heidi sped over the grass to hug Clara. Grandmamma dismounted and greeted Heidi, then turned to Grandfather. "What a magnificent place to live!" she exclaimed.

Grandfather spread some rugs on the wheelchair, lifted Clara in his strong arms, and gently settled her into it. Straightaway, Heidi pushed the wheelchair round the hut to show Clara the fir trees and the goat stall and the flowers that grew all around.

"Oh, Heidi!" cried Clara. "If only I could run about with you."

"Don't worry," said Heidi, "I'll push you everywhere."

Grandfather fetched out the table and chairs and they sat eating toasted cheese and drinking great mugs of milk in the gentle breeze.

After the meal, Heidi took Grandmamma inside the hut.
Grandfather carried Clara up the ladder to Heidi's bedroom. "Oh,
Heidi," she cried, "I never imagined such a lovely place to sleep!
Fancy being able to lie in bed and look at the stars."

Grandfather glanced at Grandmamma. "Why not leave
Clara with us for a time while you stay in the nearby
village of Ragaz?" he suggested. "I promise to look after
her, and you can come and visit whenever you please."

Clara and Heidi were overjoyed at the idea, and
Grandmamma beamed at Grandfather. "I was
thinking myself how much good it
would do Clara to stay here. What a
kind fellow you are!"

With that Grandmamma set off,
and Heidi and Clara helped
Grandfather prepare supper.

*"They've come! They've
come!" cried Heidi.*

The days with Clara passed quickly. Grandfather grew very fond of her, and he tried to find something new every day to make her better. He instructed Peter to let Daisy feed on the very best grass so she would give extra good milk to make Clara strong. Then, when Clara had been there for a fortnight, Grandfather began trying to get her on her feet. At first she gave up quickly because it hurt, but each day she tried for a little longer.

Heidi told Clara about the pasture where Peter took the goats and begged Grandfather to take them there.

"I will if Clara tries to stand on her own this evening," he smiled.

Heidi rushed to tell Peter. "We're coming up to the pasture with you tomorrow."

But Peter only growled and hit the ground with his stick. Heidi had not been to the pasture once that summer, and now she was only coming to show it to her new friend. He wished Clara would go away so that everything would be the way it was before.

When he went up to the hut the next morning, Peter saw Clara's empty wheelchair waiting outside. No-one was around. In a sudden burst of rage, he sent it plunging down the steep slope. Then he dashed up the mountain without Dusky and Daisy.

Grandfather and Heidi came out of the hut a few moments later and searched everywhere for the chair. Then Grandfather looked down the mountain and saw it in pieces a long way below.

Peter pushed the wheelchair down the mountainside.

Clara slowly put one foot in front of the other.

"It must have been the wind," said Heidi.

"Now I won't ever be able to go up to the pasture," wailed Clara.

"We'll go up anyway," said Grandfather, and then he remarked, thoughtfully, "Peter is very late."

Grandfather picked up Clara and an armful of rugs and they began the trek up to the pasture with Dusky and Daisy. Peter was already there. Grandfather scolded him for leaving the goats behind and asked, "Did you see Clara's chair?" Peter shook his head.

Grandfather left Clara and Heidi in a sunny place on the grass, where they spent the morning as happy as can be. After lunch, Heidi thought of the meadow higher up. "Oh, you must come with me to see the flowers, Clara," she said. "I'm sure Peter and I could carry you."

Peter felt so guilty that he agreed to help. They hauled Clara to her feet, and slowly but surely she began to put one foot in front of the other. "Look at me!" she cried. "I'm walking!"

When Grandfather came to collect them late that afternoon, his face lit up at the news. But Peter went home with a heavy heart. He was terrified when he saw villagers standing round the broken wheelchair.

Peter is so jealous of Clara's friendship with Heidi that he pushes her chair down the slope. Without her chair, Clara tries even harder to walk.

The next day, Clara and Heidi wrote to Grandmamma and begged her to come and see them in a week's time. They didn't say why. Clara spent all week practising her walking, until the big day finally arrived.

The girls sat down outside the hut to wait for Grandmamma in a state of great excitement. At last, she came into view. When the old lady saw the children, she cried out, "Why Clara, where's your chair?" and as she came towards them, she said, "How well you look!" Then Heidi stood up – and so did Clara, and they walked before her. Grandmamma stared in amazement. Half laughing, half crying, she hugged Clara, then Heidi, then Clara again. Seeing Grandfather, she turned to him and said, "How can we ever thank you! It's your care that has done this."

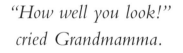

"How well you look!"
cried Grandmamma.

"And God's good sun and His mountain air," added Grandfather.

Grandmamma decided to send a telegram telling Clara's father to come immediately. "I shan't tell him why," she said.

Grandfather whistled for Peter to deliver it. Almost at once, Peter came running down from the mountain, white as a sheet. He feared that the awful moment had come when he would be arrested. He was greatly relieved to find he only had to deliver a message.

As he was running down the path to the village, a man beckoned to him. Peter stopped in his tracks but wouldn't go near. "Come along, lad," shouted the poor traveller. "Can you tell me if this path

Clara blossoms under Grandfather's good care. The fresh mountain air and healthy food have given her the strength to walk again.

leads to the hut where the old man lives with a child called Heidi, and where some people from Frankfurt are staying?"

"A *policeman!*" thought Peter. He was so terrified that he dashed off down the mountain, tripped, went head over heels, and landed in a bush.

"How shy these mountain folk are!" Mr Sesemann said to himself, and continued on his way.

He had finished his business trip early and was planning to surprise Clara by landing unexpectedly on Grandfather's doorstep.

Peter, in the meantime, had lost Grandmamma's telegram and was scrambling back up the mountain as fast as his bruises and his guilty conscience would let him go. He wanted to run and hide under his bed, but Grandfather had told him to hurry back to look after the goats, and he didn't dare disobey the old man's orders.

Peter was so terrified that he dashed off down the mountain and tripped.

Mr Sesemann chuckled when he saw Grandfather's hut a little way above him. "What a surprise they'll have when they see me!"

But he had already been spotted. An excited group stood outside the hut waiting to surprise him instead. As he drew nearer, two girls came towards him, a tall fair one leaning slightly on a smaller dark one. He stood still and stared, and suddenly his eyes filled with tears.

"Don't you know me?" Clara cried.

At that, he strode towards her and took her in his arms. "Is it possible?" he cried.

Grandmamma joined them. "Come and meet Heidi's grandfather."

Mr Sesemann thanked Grandfather with all his heart for restoring Clara's health.

While they were talking, Grandmamma saw Peter trying to slip past. "Young man," she called. "Why are you so frightened to come near us?"

Peter stared at the ground, looking ashamed.

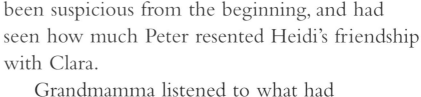

Mr Sesemann took Clara in his arms.

"I think you'll find Peter was the 'wind' that blew Clara's chair away," said Grandfather suddenly. He had been suspicious from the beginning, and had seen how much Peter resented Heidi's friendship with Clara.

Grandmamma caught Peter trying to slip past.

Grandmamma listened to what had happened, and took Peter aside. "What you did was very bad," she said, "but I understand what you must have been feeling. Now, I want you to choose something to remember us by."

Peter couldn't believe he could choose anything he liked. He thought and thought, then asked for a penny. Grandmamma laughed, and promised him a penny a week for the rest of his life. Peter thanked her and skipped off joyfully.

Later, Mr Sesemann said quietly to Grandfather, "Is there any way in which I can show you my gratitude?"

"I, too, am overjoyed at Clara's recovery," said Grandfather. "But if you could promise me that when I die you will take care of Heidi, that would richly reward me." Mr Sesemann gave his word and the two men shook hands on it.

All too soon, the time had come for Mr Sesemann, Clara, and Grandmamma to leave. Clara began to cry, but Heidi said brightly, "It'll soon be summer again and then you'll come back, and you'll be walking right from the beginning. Just think what good times we'll have!"

Heidi stood at the edge of the slope and waved goodbye till they were out of sight.

Nor was that all. Shortly afterwards, the doctor retired and came to live in the village. He bought the ramshackle house that Grandfather and Heidi had lived in, and had it rebuilt so that he could live in one half and they could use the other half in the winter.

"I have come to love Heidi almost like my own child," the doctor told Grandfather one day. "May I help you take care of her?"

Grandfather took the doctor's hand in his, and said, "That would be wonderful!"

So Heidi spent another happy winter in the village, surrounded by all those who cared for her. ❋

The doctor offered to help take care of Heidi.

Heidi's Mountain Home

HEIDI'S STORY BEGINS when she goes to live with her grandfather in the mountains in Switzerland. Life with Grandfather is simple and carefree. Heidi spends her days outdoors in the fresh air, tending the goats with Peter and helping Grandfather with his chores.

❀ MOUNTAIN VILLAGE

Grandfather lives high up in a mountain range called the Alps, and rarely goes down to the village below. The villagers gossip about him because they don't understand his ways.

❀ VILLAGE CHILDREN

In summer, village girls helped with household tasks, while boys worked on the land or, like Peter, tended sheep and goats. In the winter, children were free to attend school. Because she lives so far away, Heidi can only go to school when Grandfather moves down to the village.

It snows a lot in the Alps in winter. The only way to reach remote huts like Grandfather's was with a sled or on skis.

❋ MOUNTAIN HOME
Grandfather's hut has only one room, so Heidi has to sleep in the hayloft. It is simply furnished, and like this one, has a log fire for cooking and heating.

Milk pail

Ladle

Bowl

Grandfather toasts cheese for Heidi using a long, wooden fork.

❋ CARPENTER
In mountain areas, wood was used to build homes and make household objects. Many village men made their own furniture and utensils out of wood, like Grandfather does.

❋ WHOLESOME FOOD
Mountain people ate simple but healthy food, such as soup, brown bread, and cheese. Like many villagers, Grandfather makes his own cheese from goats' milk. He sells the cheese in the village so he can buy brown bread and meat.

The cheesemaker went from farm to farm helping to make cheese.

Goats are fearless climbers, well-adapted to the mountains.

Clara's City Home

HEIDI GOES TO STAY with Clara in the busy German city of Frankfurt. Clara's family is rich, and they live in a big house that has many rules. Heidi finds it hard to remember all of these, and she often does things that horrify Miss Rottenmeier. Heidi is often indoors, and misses the freedom and fresh air of her mountain home.

Most of the time, children were expected to remain silent unless spoken to.

The nursemaid helped the housekeeper to look after the children.

Grandmothers often lived with or visited their families.

The master of the house sat at the head of the table.

✹ FAMILY MEALTIME

Wealthy families had servants to serve meals and do the housework.
In Clara's house there is a housekeeper, a butler, a maid, and a coachman.
A cook makes rich foods with much meat and fish. Heidi is
overwhelmed by all this, and doesn't know how she should behave.

It took two days to travel between Heidi's village and Frankfurt.

✳ FRANKFURT

Heidi has never been to a city before, and cannot understand why there are buildings all around. She feels trapped inside Clara's house because she can't see the sky or the mountains. Clara tries to make Heidi feel at home.

✳ CITY HOME

Clara's family lives in a big Frankfurt house with many rooms, including a dining-room, a sitting room, and a study. This is a big change for Heidi, who is used to Grandfather's one-room hut.

✳ HOUSEKEEPER

Well-off children were often looked after by a housekeeper, such as Miss Rottenmeier. She is in charge of running the household, seeing to Clara's education, and making sure she learns her manners.

✳ TUTOR

Only rich families could afford a tutor like Mr Usher. He teaches Clara reading, writing, and maths. After a difficult start, he teaches Heidi how to read, too.

Johanna Spyri

JOHANNA SPYRI WAS BORN IN 1827, in the small Swiss village of Hirzel. Just like Heidi, she and her five brothers and sisters lived a healthy, outdoor life in the mountains. She tended the family's goats, and sometimes helped her father, who was a country doctor.

*Johanna Spyri
(1827–1901)*

The old schoolhouse in Hirzel

Heidi *was written to help men wounded in war.*

❊ WRITING FOR CHILDREN

After she married in 1852, Johanna Spyri began writing children's books to earn money to help the men wounded in the Franco-Prussian War. In 1880, her first novel, *Heidi*, was published. It was a big success. Spyri wrote almost 50 other books, but none was as well-loved as *Heidi*.

❊ A POPULAR STORY

Heidi was translated into English in 1884 and soon became popular all over the world. It inspired several film versions: in 1937, Shirley Temple starred as Heidi, and in 1952, Elspeth Sigmund played the same role.

Shirley Temple

Elspeth Sigmund